CW00336148

The Martial Handbook

By Jeremy Lesniak

Copyright 2019, All Rights Reserved

The Martial Artist's Handbook

Copyright 2019, Whistlekick, LLC

All rights reserved. No part of this book may be reproduced, stored in a retrieval system, transmitted, or similar in any form, at any time, by any process – electronic, mechanical, photocopying, recording or otherwise – without the prior written permission of the copyright owners. Any scanning, uploading, and/or distribution of this work via internet or any other means, even those not yet in existence, is illegal and punishable by law.

Dedication

This book is dedicated to everyone who has helped whistlekick grow to what it is today. You are too many to name, and for that, I am eternally grateful.

~jeremy

Thank You

Thank you to all the guests and supporters who have put Martial Arts Radio on the map. It is through this outlet that we continue to grow and reach more traditional martial artists throughout the world.

Thank you to Julius, Lessy, and Lester for your help with the episodes, and for keeping me on track.

To Steve, Mike, Liz and Alyssa – thank you for your help with editing. Special thanks to Jenni for her extraordinary efforts. It would not have happened without your selfless dedication of time.

Medical Disclaimer

Sections of this book make recommendations for training, rehabilitation and more. Understand that Jeremy Lesniak is not a doctor and holds no formal medical training. Any advice you follow based on this book should be done with discretion and under the advice and supervision of a physician.

Content Disclaimer

All aspects of this work are original. Any resemblance to work belonging to others is accidental. All quotes are attributed to the author.

Contents

Author's Introduction

This has been quite the adventure. Back in 2010 I founded a little martial arts company named whistlekick. It took several years before we produced our first products, and it wasn't until 2015 we started our podcast, Martial Arts Radio. Now, as I write this four and a half years later, we've produced over 450 episodes, with listeners in over 150 countries.

I started conceptualizing this book in 2017. My idea was to take some of the concepts from the show and write about them. To expand on details that needed expansion and to add ideas where they were lacking the first time.

What this book has turned into is something much more. First off, it's far larger than I ever imagined. Over 50,000 words. I didn't intend for that to happen, but then again, I rarely do things in a small way. I've gone back over every episode of the show, and hand-chosen topics for this book. Topics that made sense in written form, on subjects that would appeal to most martial artists, regardless of style.

Since the launch of the company, it's been dedicated to tearing down the barriers that separate martial artists. We have far more that binds us than separates us, and it is my sincere hope that this book fosters that notion.

What is written here can be but is not required to be, read in order. It is a living document – one that will be updated. It is my hope that each time we release an update, you'll read through it again. My thoughts and opinions change, and yours should, too. We cannot grow without change, and thus this book – and all the projects I work on – cannot improve without change.

If you're familiar with the podcast, the subjects in this book will be familiar. However, I re-wrote every single chapter. This is not a simple cut and paste of the audio transcripts from the show. Some of what I say here is different than when I first brought the subject to audio. Again, change is required for growth.

If nothing else, thank you for reading and for supporting this effort.

Jeremy Lesniak

Part 1 - What is Martial Arts?

Defining a Martial Art

Whenever I talk about a subject, I like to understand the definition. What is the thing that we are talking about? Because if you're going to have discussions, conversations, or debates on a subject, it is helpful when everyone is on the same page, or at least understands where people differ on their definitions. This book is about martial arts, so it is important that we talk about what is a martial art and what is not, and to give you inspiration to decide how you define martial arts, I am going to offer my definition of what is a martial art.

There are two ways that we can look at this definition. We can look at the way the combined use of the two words have come to have meaning in our societies, and we can break down the construct of the term "martial art." The two have similar definitions for a lot of people and for me, but they are not necessarily the same.

My definition of martial arts is, "a practice that offers personal development through the idea, the perspective, the lens of combat." When we look at this definition, it becomes straightforward to decide what is and is not a martial art. Soccer is not a martial art, even if you decide that there is personal development happening because there is no combat aspect. There is no practice, real or imagined, involving a fight.

This also starts to explain why some things that are maybe unique to traditional martial arts are let go of when working toward more focused combat pursuits. Boxing and wrestling, for example, are often debated as to whether or not they are martial arts, and it comes down to not the combat aspect, but the personal development aspect. In more traditional martial arts, we have things like meditation. We have drills that are designed to do nothing more than to make us better, not necessarily better at skills, but better as people. When we look at a typical boxing or wrestling practice - and I'm not picking on these disciplines, because I think they're absolutely wonderful - not every boxing and wrestling school or coach is going to implement drills that are not directly relatable to time on the mat or in the ring, and this becomes the difference.

If we slice up the term *martial art* from a grammatical perspective, we see that the noun is *art*, and *martial* is an adjective. Martial arts are a type of art. It is a type of art that involves combat. The word martial really means, "warlike," so it is "a warlike art."

Art is the expression or application of human creative skill and imagination; thus, creativity becomes important. Freeform aspects of martial arts are a requirement based on this definition. I really like the use of the word "expression" in this definition of art because I think that is an important part of martial arts. There is an expression of who we are through our movement, whether that's in forms, or in basics, or in some fighting aspect to our training, and I think that is a critical piece. While most of us understand that it's there, we don't always talk about it.

If we put everything together that we just talked about, a martial art is, "an expressive, combat-themed practice that incorporates personal development." I am not saying that definition is unique to this book or unique to me, but it's one that I have put together through my research, through understanding what these words mean, and through my personal understanding and history with the martial arts. You can feel free to use this definition or disagree with aspects or even the entire thing. That is the beauty of coming up with a definition is that it can mean different things to different people. Thus, the subjectivity is a key factor. It makes deciding what is and is not a martial art a very personal, often debatable, hotly contested discussion.

Quite often, when we talk about martial arts, we really mean traditional martial arts, and I do make a distinction. Traditional martial arts are not limited to Asian martial arts, but that's where many people think of them as originating, and for a martial art to be traditional, it has to have some sort of historical significance. We'll talk about that more in the next section of this book.

Even though I have put forth a definition of martial arts here, I'm not sure how convinced I am that it is a correct or accurate definition, even within my understanding. I have discussions with people all the time about what is and is not a martial art. For example, Krav Maga is often seen as not a martial art by many, but it certainly fits the definition of personal development, and there is certainly a strong combat aspect there as displayed in the way it is trained in the schools that I have experienced. Also, consider that boxing to some is not a martial art because it often lacks the sometimes-mystical quality, that introspective, internal aspect that a lot of martial arts have. Yet, to some, boxing is one of the oldest martial arts. You can see why it is difficult to compose one universally applicable definition for martial arts.

I'm not here to tell you what you should think a martial art is or is not. I simply want you to consider what the term martial arts means *to you*. As you come up with your own definition, it may change. As you read through this book, I want you to see how your definition may shift, or how your definition may help you understand some of the subjects that we're going to get into.

Traditional Martial Arts vs Modern Martial Arts

In the last section, I referred to martial arts, but I also specified traditional martial arts. What other kinds of martial arts are there? A lot of people make a distinction between traditional martial arts and modern martial arts, sometimes used with another M-word, mixed martial arts. This book isn't going to talk specifically about mixed martial arts, MMA. This is something we avoid doing at whistlekick, not because I don't respect MMA, and not because I dislike MMA. I'll watch MMA. I have friends who are practitioners and friends who are professional fighters, and I think the world of them and what they do, but there is a difference between traditional martial arts - which some people abbreviate as TMA - and MMA.

What are those differences? The biggest differences come down to the definitions and what is important. In traditional martial arts, the value is generally on the personal development side, whether or not it is explicitly articulated. You can have an absolutely wonderful traditional martial arts practitioner, someone who is a great instructor, someone who is a fantastic student, with wonderful technique and balance in their forms, and they can also be a horrible fighter. They could get their butt kicked in a simple mugging 100 times out of 100. That same person would not be defined as a great or even passable MMA fighter.

In mixed martial arts, the value is on combat skills. That's not to say that people who train in MMA don't also derive development benefits, or that they don't become better people as they train, but not all of them do. There are even some schools that will teach MMA in a way that, I think, sends people backwards down the personal development spectrum. People become often lesser versions of themselves as they become better fighters. ` Maybe I shouldn't say often. Maybe I should say sometimes, but the fact that progress in mixed martial arts is not lockstep with personal development, that is the difference for me between MMA and TMA.

Why does it matter that the two are different? Why am I spending time in this book to offer my definition and draw a line between the two of them? Because to some, martial arts means mixed martial arts, and to others, martial arts means traditional martial arts, and I think it's important as we move forward to know that in extremely little of what we will discuss in this book, am I referring to anything that is MMA-related.

This does not mean that if you practice a blended traditional martial arts style that I'm throwing stones at you. It does not mean that I don't see the value in practicing combat skills for the sake of practicing combat skills. I have trained with and befriended some amazing MMA fighters. I have attended seminars with former UFC champions, and I've enjoyed my time. Some of these were wonderful people, and I want to make sure people understand that by drawing this line between the two things, it doesn't mean that I'm disparaging MMA. Most of you have probably heard the adage, "Fences make good neighbors." By drawing a line and understanding what exists on the traditional versus the mixed side of martial arts, we can have a more accurate, fair discussion that best represents our own personal beliefs.

The Way the World Sees Martial Arts

When we think about martial arts, it is inevitable to wonder, to contemplate the way the rest of the world sees martial artists. I have known a lot of martial artists, and I have known a lot of people who are not martial artists. I can say generally martial artists are overall better people. I'm not saying dramatically better, but I'm saying better. That is part of the reason I feel martial arts is for everyone, and that everyone should do martial arts at least for a little while. I recommend six months. In training, people will become better people. They will have a better understanding of martial arts. While not everyone will stick with it, some will. And those that don't will at least have a better understanding of what martial arts is, and carry that out into the world. They will be better people, and they'll ultimately help spread the martial arts, whether that's through friends, family, children, or just innocent bystanders who hear their stories.

As a rule, I think the rest of the world sees martial arts practitioners as positive, stable, reliable people, that are a good influence on others. That is why so many people want to put their children in martial arts classes even if they've never done martial arts themselves. Therefore, even in busy times, with competition from extracurricular sports like soccer and whatnot, parents are willing to bring their children to martial arts classes, not because of the physical benefits, but because of the inherent personal development, the growth that accompanies martial arts training. The world sees that, they understand that, and they are willing to value it.

One of the questions I receive from time to time is about putting martial arts on a resume, and yes, the optimistic way the rest of the world views us does warrant adding martial arts credentials to your resume or CV. If you hold a black belt or maybe have achieved some national championships in competition, I think those can go on a resume as they demonstrate qualities like perseverance and dedication that set you apart as a martial artist. Sometimes people will question that. They'll ask me, "But, what if a place of employment doesn't want to hire me because they think I might be violent?" Let's face it, if martial arts are a big part of your life, and the culture of that place of employment doesn't understand martial arts, and they would reject you for it, is that a place you want to work? It's not somewhere I would want to be.

For the most part, the rest of the world sees us in a positive light, but several things happen that don't exactly help that situation. One of those issues, those problems, is the ego that so many martial artists showcase. Don't get me wrong, by numbers, I don't think that most martial artists have excessive egos, but the problem with ego is that ego begets attention, and thus we start to see martial artists with large egos seeking attention. Those are the people that, regrettably, the rest of the world sees.

Unfortunately, as social media grows, as it becomes easier to find news online, and as the world woefully shifts towards negativity, we start to see more and more showcase of martial artists doing bad things, saying bad things, and the world is noticing. I don't think it's had a dramatic impact yet, but it may if we don't start policing our own, if we don't start speaking up as good people against the bad people - and I don't mean martial artists who have questionable rank, or dubious business practices, or their self-defense instruction might be subpar. I mean people who are molesting children. I mean people who are outright stealing or are engaged in crime. Those are the people we need to stand up and speak out against, or we're going to lose this favorable perception that we hold in the world.

If you break down the term martial arts, you'll see that the noun, the core of the phrase, is actually art. It's not about learning to fight, it's about learning to be better through the expression of action.

Part 2 –Martial Art Styles, Schools & Instructors

Cross Training

If you spend much time in martial arts, at some point you'll have a conversation with someone about the idea of cross training, that is, training in something that is not the primary martial art that you have chosen. This concept has become so popular that many martial arts schools offer if automatically. While anyone just coming into martial arts might think, "Oh, this is a great idea. Work on more than one thing at a time," it is a far more nuanced conversation, and it can cause some problems.

When we talk about cross training, we compare the notions of *diversity* of training versus *mastery* of training, which are two opposing ends of the same spectrum. The analogy of a spectrum with two endpoints is merely an intellectual exercise to illustrate these concepts. None of us are ever training in only one style, or all styles, for the sheer fact that each style is made up of other styles, and every instructor has taken some ideas from someone else somewhere along the way. There is no purity of martial arts anymore, and anyone that says otherwise is probably being foolish.

When we talk about mastery of a single martial arts style, we are talking about remaining in the same style, perhaps even in the same school and under the same instructor, for a long period of time. You can focus your training on making improvements to a limited curriculum, with the goal of mastering your art. If you find the word "mastering" or "mastery" unacceptable, perhaps "competency" would be more appropriate. When we think about that mastery, that competency, we are looking at the idea that there are fewer things to do, so you can apply more effort to each of those things. Fewer techniques, fewer forms, and as we dig into them, we can become better at each of them.

Every martial art, no matter where it comes from or who teaches it, has a lot of nuances. There are numerous intricacies in each style, and not all of them can be taught. Some of it must be discovered, experienced, as you become a higher rank and invest more and more time training. The less time you have, the less likely you are to discover some of these aspects of martial arts. In other words, the more time you spend cross training, pursuing that diversity, the less likely you are to find these hidden gems.

However, diversity can help invigorate your passion for training. It can give you new ideas, new experiences, new lessons that you can take from one style and apply to others. When we look at the best fighters, whether that be in a particular martial arts style or mixed martial arts, they tend to have cross trained. They have diversity in their martial arts training. If you want to be a great fighter, you probably want to be a diverse fighter.

The downside to diversity is that you are less likely to develop a high level of skill, a high level of competency. You are probably not going to reach your full potential in a single style if you're training in more than one martial art as it will limit your ability to invest time in training in any one style. If your goal is personal growth, sticking with a single style is probably going to yield better results over time.

You can take anything too far. Diversity can go too far when you spend so much time training in so many things that you don't develop even basic competency in any of them. The idea of mastery goes too far when you become so focused that you ignore what is going on around you, perhaps even remaining blind to some of the ways the techniques you are training are not working for you.

To figure out which makes sense for you - and again, these are not black and white options, there's a whole shade of grey here - you have to figure out your "why." Why are you training? What are your goals? What's important to you? The sooner you can find your "why," the sooner you can figure out how best to approach the dilemma - and trust me, it does become a dilemma - of diversity versus mastery.

If and when you choose to learn additional arts, whether that be simultaneous with one or after, you'll want to remember your "why," and you'll want to understand what is different. What's different in the system, what's different in the school I'm training in, what's different with the instructor? By understanding the differences, you can better understand all the things that you're training and how they relate to both you and your "why."

Children in Martial Arts

The martial arts are great for children. It has even become a bit of a cliché. If you look at the enrollment at most martial arts schools, it is overwhelmingly children. In some areas, training in martial arts as a child is almost a rite of passage. It's something that children look forward to, especially in their earlier years before they reach team sports.

There are several reasons why martial arts is beneficial for children. It is beneficial both physically and mentally. It can be a great avenue to avoid obesity and build healthier habits. It can build focus and positively develop attitudes. The most often cited reason is martial arts can build confidence and self-esteem.

Martial arts instructors occupy this odd middle ground between schoolteachers and parents. Martial arts instructors are not legally prohibited from doing certain things that schoolteachers are. Martial arts instructors can help parents with imposing discipline on their children, giving them a strong figure to look up to in a way that public school teachers can't get away with. In some cases, children at certain ages tend to be more positively influenced by schoolteachers or martial arts instructors than their parents. This makes martial arts a wonderful avenue for parents to continue to seek development and positive role modeling for their children.

How can you build a successful youth martial arts program? It comes down to a couple of things: handing out discipline with love and handing out love with discipline. Children need to know that when they are disciplined, they are also loved. I'm using the term love a little bit differently than we might if we were talking about parents and children, but the best martial arts instructors I know have love for their students and the arts, and it comes through. It's obvious how they feel, how much they enjoy what they do, and how core it is to their being to do it.

The strictness of the discipline, the standards to which the students are held is related to their age and their rank. This is something that tends to happen innately, and it's easier to effect when youth classes are broken up by both age and rank. Depending on the size of your enrollment, that can be difficult, but don't underestimate the effectiveness.

Not every martial art is great for every child. Some children will do better based on grappling arts. Some children will do better based on striking arts. Some children are better off with the strictness of certain Okinawan and Japanese disciplines, while others need a much more energetic, fluid, free-thinking environment. To understand what makes a martial arts program unique and beneficial is paramount to attracting the right students and making sure that they are retained and receive the benefit that they need.

Not everyone is going to fit into a particular martial arts school. Different martial arts instructors conduct their programs differently, which will work better or worse for different children. This is why it's so important that martial arts instructors be willing to refer children who don't quite fit their mold to other nearby schools.

There are a lot of great ways to build a youth program, and some absolutely wonderful experts out in the industry who can help you do that, and that is far beyond the scope of what is intended not only in this chapter but in this book.

Different Martial Arts Styles

There are many, many different martial arts styles. When we start to think about them, it can be human nature to think about the history of each, when, and why they originated. While there is some importance to history, there is also the relevance to what we do today. Thinking about it in another way, it doesn't matter what style came first or which styles come from which other styles because that causes separation, it causes division, and if you know anything about me, you know I'm not a fan of divvying up martial arts.

Whenever you talk about something that gets broken up into different groups, people want to know which is best, which one is superior, and in a way, this has been tested time and again, but with different results. Not only is there no clear answer, I think the question is flawed, even foolish, because it is so subjective. "Best" is a very subjective notion, and it is based entirely on what your goal is, what your "why" is. Some styles may be better or worse for someone based on their build, taller versus shorter, for example. The best style for personal growth, well, that doesn't exist because it's up to the instructor and the way that art is taught, so I don't like getting trapped into these conversations about which is best.

When you look online, or you look at a group of martial artists having this conversation, this debate, really what it comes down to is that some martial artists are afraid to face the fact that their martial arts style, their training, the thing they have invested so much time into may not be the best for them based on their "why." That leaves people arguing and fighting and coming up with reasons why one thing is better than another. I look at it differently. We don't just *have* different martial arts; we *need* them. Different people need different things out of martial arts. We have different bodies, we have different "whys," and different schools, systems, and instructors are going to help us achieve our "why" easier than others. It is, in a sense, a marketing maneuver for us as martial artists to have different options for the people training.

The more diverse the options, the more likely someone will find what they want. I think most martial artists would agree that we want people training martial arts rather than not. Even if we have a style, a school, an instructor that we love passionately, we would rather have someone training elsewhere than not at all. I believe that is paramount. That is why I founded whistlekick, to grow and spread the traditional martial arts.

At the end of the day, there are a limited number of ways that you can move the body. When you are considering combat, martial arts, self-defense, whatever you want to call it, only a small percentage of the ways that we can move the body make any sense. When you think about it, martial arts styles are far more alike than they are different.

We have more styles today than we used to as people break off and form their own concepts, codify them, and call them "style." Some people point at that and they think it's somewhere between foolish or disrespectful. I don't see it that way. I think it's just people exploring their own personal martial arts, their own personal philosophies, their own personal understanding, and I think that's great.

You can't have progress without change. Nothing that we are doing is perfect, and there is always an opportunity for further growth. People who refuse that change are either lazy or afraid. There is always another way, there is always a better way, but sometimes you must dig deep and let go of your ego. It is our responsibility to keep the martial arts going. To allow styles to evolve and adapt is critical, and it's something that a lot of us need to be more willing to do.

There is nothing better to me than a martial artist considering what makes them a martial artist, what makes them tick, and what works for them, because that gives an opportunity for us to work together, to train together, to have intelligent and rational conversation, even debate about what works or doesn't work for each of us. The more we collaborate, the more we can accomplish.

Finding the Right Martial Arts School

When we talk about people finding the right school, inevitably someone is going to come to some martial artist and ask them, "Where should I train? What style should I train in?" Most people seem to get this wrong. What they do provides a disservice to the martial arts and the people who come to them for this advice.

When people come to us and ask which martial art is best for them, or what martial art school should they attend, instead of simply answering from our own experience and viewpoint, we must ask questions. Anyone in sales knows this is part of the qualification process. You have to know what people need before you can sell them.

The first question you should ask is, what is available to this individual? If someone comes to you and they say, "What martial art should I do?" and you say, "Goju-Ryu karate," and there's no Goju-Ryu karate school in their area, guess what? They're not going to train in anything. If you know anything about me, I've said it in this book before, I've said it on our podcast, I've said it all over the place, I believe people are better off taking *any* martial art than *no* martial art.

When people want to know what martial art they should take, help them understand their options. If they have three or four different choices, help them understand what questions to ask of the instructors. Encourage them to visit the schools and observe classes. Help them figure out how much time they're going to dedicate to it and what their goals are. All martial art schools are not created equal. All instructors are different, and styles are different because people's needs and wants can be very different.

As with most things in martial arts, when you are helping people, it's important to drop your ego. The martial art that you study is not the only option. Even if you run a school, which would you rather have: a student to come in, spend six weeks with you, and then drop out with a bad relationship to martial arts because it wasn't a good fit; or would you rather that they go down the street, train for a few years, find that they want something different, and now with new context for what martial arts is, they come to you, they train with you, and they stick around for a much longer time?

We all like to take pride in the things that we do and the choices that we make, so it makes sense that people are proud of the martial arts school that they run or simply train in. When we tell people that, "My school is best," or, "My martial art is best," "The place I go to is the absolute best," we are turning people off. We're making them concerned. People don't like to make wrong or bad decisions. If they're out looking for a martial arts school, and they ask people, "Where should I go?" and they get conflicting answers, they are more likely to make *no* decision. We live in a busy time. People look for excuses to not do things. If someone is not sure what choice is the right choice for them, they would rather make no decision, because that way they're not wrong, and they can spend their time, their money, their passion on something other than martial arts.

Find out why people want to train. People have different "whys." Some people want to train for self-defense, some for fitness, some for a social outlet. Others simply want to become better people. They want that personal development side. These are all great answers. There's no wrong answer to this question, but understanding the answer is imperative to helping connect a potential martial arts student with an appropriate school.

What experience do they have with martial arts? Is it only from watching television and movies, or have they trained in the past, maybe even recently? If someone left a martial arts school, understanding why they left is critical. Find out how long they're willing to travel. How much time do they want to train? Do they want to train twice a week? Three times a week? Six times a week? Different schools offer different options. Matching up people with schools that meet their wants and needs creates lifelong relationships with martial arts.

Whether you're a student, school owner, or an instructor, don't be afraid to sell your school if it is a proper fit, but don't get hurt if it's not chosen. Instead of saying bad things about other martial arts schools, share the positives about yours. Help them build a sense of community right away. This is not the old days. This is not life or death. We're not part of clans that need to war with each other to prove whose martial art is better. The more people have positive feelings about you and the school that you train at or the school you own, the more likely they are to stick around. People want to belong to something positive, something that makes them feel good. Make sure that they feel good about your school right away.

Keep in mind, you don't know everyone in the martial arts community in your area. I'm constantly surprised at how in small-town Vermont I find out about new schools down the road that I never even knew about or someone teaching out of their basement, garage, or a church. They may not be large, they may not have lots of students, but they're still serving the good. They're still providing martial arts to people. I don't assume that I know all the options. I encourage people who are interested in training to talk to others, to have the same conversation with fellow martial artists that they're having with me.

If you're looking at training somewhere else, if you're moving to a new area or the martial arts school you're part of is no longer a good fit, all of these questions are still appropriate. Maybe you could ask them of yourself. Do the research. Figure out what's important to you, what's not important to you, and what's going to provide the best fit. Whether it's going to be the only school you train in, or maybe you're cross training in a second or third school, all of these questions, all of these decisions are important to understand so you or the people you're talking to can find the best martial arts fit for them, so they can develop a positive lifelong relationship with their training.

Everyone is a Teacher

Everyone has something to teach, but just having something to teach does not make you a teacher. Being a teacher is a lot more. It's a responsibility and an undertaking. You are taking the weight of the education of the people that you're working with; you are carrying that on your shoulders, and you have made that a priority for you. When you look at teaching, whether it is in the martial arts or outside of martial arts, you can see that the best teachers do this. Unfortunately, some martial arts instructors really don't care that much about the development of their students. Conversely, we have plenty of martial arts instructors who do, and even some who care maybe a bit too much.

In martial arts, teachers are revered. We value their knowledge, and we value them because of their knowledge. As a student, regardless of what you do, the moment you open yourself, it is important to set aside your pride, your ego, so you can receive as much as you can from the people with whom you are training.

Everyone has a teacher, or at least should. It may not be a formal relationship, you may not be advancing in rank, and in fact, you may simply be watching YouTube videos, but if you're open to learning, even if you cannot articulate who the individual or group of people are, you have a teacher. You are learning. If you are a student, teachers are guiding you.

Sometimes people advance in rank and they lose their instructors. Maybe they die off, or maybe they have a disagreement and they branch out on their own. In those cases, sometimes people do not take on a new teacher. They work through their own movements. They progress by analyzing things on their own, maybe in a mirror or on video. They study. They reflect. In this scenario, you are not your own teacher. You are still a student, but you are practicing. Practicing is of course important. It's refining, it's making you better, and that is critical, but the ceiling on where you can progress to has a lot to do with your time with a teacher. If you are not progressing, you are not developing, and there is less that you have to share with your students, or with the world in general.

Martial artists without an instructor of their own cannot truly become better. Everything they are working from, everything they are practicing is coming from their own knowledge. You may achieve competency, you may refine your skill, but you are still working from the same body of understanding. I believe everyone needs a teacher to guide growth and personal development.

Development is the key to martial arts. It is the underpinning of everything that we do. Its why martial arts is so wonderful. Development means new information, new knowledge. The very best martial artists, regardless of their rank, their accomplishments, they still have teachers and are still learning. I've trained with the best martial artists in the world, and every one of them looks to others for new knowledge. Sometimes we refer to that as "the white belt   mentality." One of the many beautiful characteristics of martial arts is that you never stop learning; there is always something new. No matter your rank, no matter your skill, no matter how many black belts you have, to put on a white belt, literally or figuratively, will make you better. I think it is an important, even critical, part of martial arts overall.

One of the challenges that people have brought to me is around their own education, the feeling that they are not learning anything new, that they are not developing. This typically happens with people in the second, third, and fourth degree black belt ranks. Often, they are spending their time teaching, and they can sometimes feel left out, that their instructor has not shared new wisdom. In some systems you learn the entire curriculum for your first-degree black belt, which can leave you wondering, "What else is there to learn?" There *is* a tremendous amount to learn, and sometimes you can learn the most while you are instructing others.

What we have talked about in this chapter is education. It's about teaching, and it's about learning. If everyone is a teacher, then everyone is a student, and as you advance in rank, it is important to know what role you are in at any given time. Honestly, the very best teachers that I've worked with are students every moment that they are teachers. If you've spent much time teaching people, especially young children, you've likely learned something about things that you've never expected to learn. Whether you are a teacher, student, or both, the key to being the best at each is being open.

The beauty of martial arts is that gives back exactly, and only, what you put in.

Part 3 – Physical Considerations

Overview

While much of the world does not look at martial arts and martial artists and think of people that practice these amazing disciplines as being athletes, martial artists push the boundaries of what is physically possible in a way that very few other people do. For years, and as long as the internet has been around, we have seen videos of martial artists doing incredible things. We watch martial artists put their hands and feet through large blocks of concrete or significant amounts of wood and demonstrate physical strength and power that you would typically see in powerlifters or others who pursue a physical, powerful, strength-based sport. We see trickers, people throwing jumping-spinning-kicking combinations that are on the level of many Olympic gymnasts. We see martial artists move their hands and feet so quickly that it can be difficult to watch. Martial arts addresses and practices all the various types of physical development that you could imagine, from strength, to speed, to balance, and a complete martial artist has addressed and worked on all these physical development aspects.

As you progress as a martial artist, you must take control of your body. You have to understand not only what it *can* do, but what it *could* do. As we grow as martial artists, we tend to get faster. We tend to get stronger. Sure, as we age, we may lose some of that, but it tends to happen much, much later than a lot of people realize. I've watched people into their 60s, 70s, and even older get better at martial arts, including physically, and it blows me away. At the same time, I'm not surprised because I have been watching it happen for decades.

The more you use martial arts to develop your body, the *longer* you can use martial arts to develop your body. As you become stronger, faster, healthier through martial arts, you can continue training at a high level far longer than many people would ever pursue another physical discipline. You don't tend to see powerlifters in their 70s and 80s, but you certainly see martial artists breaking wood, sparring, and going hard into their 60s, 70s, and 80s. I've sparred with people at these ages, and I've taken some incredibly powerful shots. I am not embarrassed to say it!

The other side of considering martial arts as a physical discipline is that it must be practiced as a physical discipline. I've seen martial artists who don't progress physically. They learn how to move their body, but they don't test it, they don't challenge the movement of their body. There are people who have earned black belts and trained for 10, 20 years that can't do ten pushups, martial artists who value what the martial arts can do for them, but they haven't trained their body in such a way that they can get the most out of it. This could be due to anything from a lack of flexibility, a lack of health, or becoming or remaining overweight. I am not criticizing anyone. I am not saying these are things you have to do, but I am saying that if martial arts is important, and you want to get the most out of it, to develop as much as you can, you have to get stronger, you have to get faster, and you have to lose weight.

Let's talk about strength. Stronger muscles permit you to jump higher, jump farther, deliver more power, more force when landing a technique. If you ask your muscles to do more than they are used to, they will adapt. You'll want to progress slowly so you don't injure yourself, but muscles will get stronger, and you will get stronger if you train in the right way. Squats, jumping squats, lunges, these are some great exercises for developing strength and power, and they make you a more effective martial artist.

Pushups are probably the single best exercise for a martial artist. Just as a side note here, when you are doing pushups, point your index fingers out. Don't flare your elbows and bring your fingers in. It puts a lot of strain on the rotator muscles in your back and your shoulder, and you don't want surgery - it stinks. Another note, when you're doing pushups, touch your chest to the ground. It's far more accurate as we compare a pushup to a punch. From retracting that fist all the way, to putting it out all the way, yes, touch your chest to the ground. I know it's harder, but it will make you better. Trust me.When we talk about cardiovascular aspects to the martial arts, as you increase your stamina, you can do more, you can train harder for longer, you can spar at a higher level and remain safe and effective, and of course, that carries over into self-defense. If you want to improve your stamina in sparring, you need to practice at that same intensity. Running a 12-minute mile doesn't make you better at that high-intensity time duration of sparring. Your body has different energy systems, and if you want to perform at a certain level of intensity, you have to train at that intensity by practicing at that intensity repeatedly, making slow progress, and your body will adapt. You will have more in the tank, so to speak, and once you reach a certain threshold, you'll be amazed at how much more you can get out of your training because you can go harder for longer.

My number one drill for martial artists improving their cardiovascular stamina and their fitness: burpees. If you are not sure what a burpee is, there are 10,000 videos on the internet that you could watch. To perform a burpee, from standing, lay down as quickly as you can, then stand back up, and jump and clap your hands over your head. That's it. Very simple. Make sure you're doing it safely. If you have injuries, I don't recommend performing burpees. I probably need to throw in a medical disclaimer here that you should talk to your doctor before you do anything - you can't sue me for this - but burpees are awesome, and everyone should be doing them.

Let's talk about flexibility. If you stretch routinely, if you make it a habit, your body will adapt. It will become more flexible. In order to get real benefit out of stretching, you move slowly. You've got to be gentle. If you go too hard too fast, not only can you hurt yourself, your body may adapt in the other way, and you may build scar tissue or tense muscles that are restricting the progress that you're trying to make. You should warm-up before you stretch cold muscles. Jumping jacks, sit-ups, things that are easy for you to do without having stretched out are all good ways to bring your heart rate up.

Some people are down on ballistic stretching, the idea of carrying motion through a stretch, as opposed to static stretching where you hold the stretch, but I have found ballistic stretching to be far more applicable to martial arts, and far more beneficial. I can do a lot more in less time, but it does require me to be smart, and to know the limits of my body, and to not move too quickly or too far into the end range of where my body can move.

The Idea of Speed

Speed is critical to a martial artist. It does not matter how good your technique is, how strong it is, how powerful you are, or how perfectly you've located the target. If it's slow, it's useless. The faster you can be, the more effective you are going to be. It doesn't matter whether it is self-defense, sparring, or even your forms. The faster they are, the better we all recognize them to be. Do not confuse speed with reaction time. They are different. Reaction time is important, but speed has nothing to do with reaction time. Speed is how fast you generate your motion. Reaction time is how quickly you respond to someone else's motion.

To be truly fast, you must be relaxed. Contracted muscles are slow to move. If you watch a lot of professional combat sports, whether that be boxing or wrestling or MMA, the best athletes stay relaxed except when they absolutely need to be tense, and when they are tense, they tense only the muscles that need to be tensed.

If you have spent much time in the martial arts, you have probably spent some time training relaxation - understanding the difference between a tense muscle and a relaxed muscle, and understanding how that can affect your speed and everything else about what you do. As we get tired, fatigued, we get slower. It's natural and more reason to work on relaxing. We want to preserve that speed if humanly possible.

When we talk about raw speed, the ability to generate fast motion right away, not over the length of the technique, but from the initiation point to the impact point, we know that it stems from relaxation, and we know that it degrades over time, as you get tired. As you use those tools, they will fade. Through practice, you can use them longer, but when you must use them, whether that's in combat or sparring, you have a finite number of times that you can use those techniques at that speed.

Most of us think about this type of speed as the only speed that matters, but it's not. We have other ways that we gauge our speed that are just as - sometimes more - important. Retraction speed is the big one. More than just how fast you can hit your target, it is important to train how fast you can retract that hand, or foot, or whatever it is you are doing, so you can be ready for the next attack or defense. I like to think of it as punching and then pulling back twice as fast. Not only does it give the illusion that you're faster, but it will also oftentimes generate more force at the impact point, and you have the added benefit of being ready to go again even faster.

You can practice getting faster. It is not chaos, it is not just something you're born with, and it is not something you have to accept as-is. Speed is an adaptation of your body. It takes time to build the endurance to practice the speed, but once you can throw fast techniques a few times, you can practice throwing those techniques as quickly as possible.

Here's an example of a drill to make you faster. Set up in whatever stance you choose, maybe a fighting stance, and be ready to throw a punch with the lead hand. Relax. Don't apply any tension to anything more than what you have to, and then just once, throw that punch off the lead hand in whatever way is correct for you, for your purposes, in your style, and pull it back.

Do that as quickly as you can and do that once every 30 seconds. Do it that way for maybe five minutes. That's only 10 punches. The reason to perform the drill in this way is if you practice that punch a whole bunch of times and you start to get tired; you're not simply adapting for speed. You're adapting for endurance. If you're throwing that punch at ¾ speed, you're telling your body, "This is the speed I need to throw this at most often." If you want to get faster, you have to practice throwing that punch - or whatever the technique is - as quickly as possible and push your upper limits every time.

If you do that a few times a week, you will get faster, dramatically faster. The more you work on the accessory ideas we've talked about, like relaxation, pulling the technique back, as well as other things like breathing and having a great stance, these will help you be faster, too.

Handling Injuries

When we talk about handling injuries in the martial arts, the first thing I have to say is that I am not a doctor. I am not legally permitted to offer any official medical advice, so please consider everything I say here as unqualified information. Nearly everything I share about health and recovery in books and in podcasts comes from my own experiences.

With martial arts training, injuries are inevitable. If you are challenging your body, if you're working with other people in an intimate, physical way, you're going to get banged up. Sometimes those bumps and bruises will turn into something more severe, maybe a broken bone or two. That's part of training. No doubt you want to get better so you can get back to training so that you can resume progressing, and that requires recovering and properly healing those injuries.

The number one place where recovery happens is sleep. The better, quality sleep you get, the more you're going to heal, and the faster your body will heal. There are certainly times to power through life and avoid sleep, but when you're injured, that is not one of them. The more injured you are, the more you need sleep. When you are dealing with an injury, and you're tired, that is your body saying, "Hey! I need to rest. I need to work on healing this thing that you did to us." Maybe that means you're going to bed much earlier than usual. Maybe it means you're taking naps. Maybe it means that you're waking up later. All are okay. All are important if you want to recover as quickly as possible.

The next most important aspect of healing is food. The better the food you eat, the better you'll recover. Better quality food means your body has to do less work to process it. It means that it is using less energy to turn that food into energy, and it is instead using that extra energy on healing. The healthier you are regarding food and diet, the easier it will be for your body to recover. Your body doesn't have to do as much day-to-day work to keep it operational compared to an unhealthy body.

Through this recovery time, you should be drinking a lot of good, quality water. What is good, quality water? It obviously doesn't come out of a ditch, or a mud puddle in your driveway, but it also doesn't come out of plastic bottles. It doesn't come out of jugs that have been sitting in the sun. There is a lot of science coming out, more and more every day, showing how important water is and maybe more importantly, how significant water storage is. Ideally, you want to get your water from glass containers and from springs. If you're getting your water from home, maybe you want to filter out the fluoride and other heavy metals and minerals. There is a ton of research available on the internet and in books, and I would advise you to check that research out if this is new information to you.

Once we get beyond sleep, food, and water, we can talk about extra stuff, things like acupuncture, or massage therapy, or chiropractic care. There are entire industries of people who are out there to help you recover - physical therapists, occupational therapists, and more. Depending on your injury, your needs, and the way you recover, you may find that one or more of these people will be helpful. Don't be afraid to reach out and find some of these folks to help you get better. If one of them is not working well, that doesn't necessarily mean their modality is bad. Just because a chiropractor, for example, hasn't been helpful, doesn't mean no chiropractor will be helpful. Don't be afraid to interview multiple practitioners.

There are different grades of injury. We've been talking about severe injuries, the ones that will keep you from training. What about the lower-grade ones, the ones that you can push through? Should you? Sometimes, but not always. When we talk about low-grade injuries, sometimes we are talking about burn-out. We're talking about our body being physically unwilling to continue. It can, but it doesn't want to. I think most of us have experienced this. When you get to class and start training, and your body just isn't in it, or your heart isn't there, that might be a sign that your body is banged up and needs a break. The more intense your training, the more intense your recovery needs to be to match that. Just because you get better, and you're a higher rank, and you have more time training, that doesn't necessarily mean that your body is necessarily better at recovering.

Keep in mind, pain relievers are not cures. They don't stop anything other than the healing process. Remember, no one out there is deficient in ibuprofen. If you find that taking pain relievers is a routine part of your after-training protocol, maybe it's time to address things in a different way. There are a variety of natural pain relievers, things that are much less intense on the body, things like turmeric, or curcumin root - which is what turmeric comes from - which could be an option for you. There's a lot of research out there, and far more than we can put into a chapter in this book.

Ideally, if you have a chronic, even low-grade issue, you want to address that. Find the root cause. What is making you hurt? Find out what is creating that problem in your body and address it. The better you're able to solve these challenges, the better prepared you're going to be for training long term. The fewer injuries, the less time you'll have to take off from training, and if you become an instructor, the better you'll be able to help your students.

Ultimately, the best way to handle any injury is to prevent it. *Pre*-hab, *pre*-habilitation, this is a real thing, and it can be helpful. We all know what our weaker body parts are, those parts of our body that are more prone to injury or pain than others. There are exercises that you can do to address every single one of them. Whether we're talking about changing your shoes to account for your knees, whether we're talking about resistance training to build muscle up around your joints, or we're talking about swimming or walking as prehabilitative movement, there are a nearly infinite number of ways that you can address prehabilitation and prepare your body for training.

The best way to find out what works for you is to experiment. All those medical practitioners, physical therapists, etc., that I mentioned earlier in the chapter, by visiting those people when you do have an injury, they can give you exercises and concepts that you can work from to prevent those injuries from happening again. Don't be afraid to ask. If you have someone who is sharing a similar injury, ask them questions, find out more. It doesn't mean the root cause is the same, so you have to be careful, but the more knowledge you have and the more you explore applying the knowledge, the better off you will be because you will understand your body and you will be able to figure out what works.

Warming Up

Warming up is critical. It does not matter if you're stepping in to teach a class, to take a class, to compete, or to train on your own or with a friend. Warming up is what sets up your body for success. It helps you get the most out of your training, and it can help prevent injury.

Many, and dare I say, even most martial arts schools seem to skimp on their warm-ups. Warming up is something that happens as an afterthought. Maybe it doesn't even happen in every class. I think that's risky. Not only does it put people at greater risk for injury, but it also doesn't allow them to get as much out of the workout as they could. I understand the thought process behind this decision if you only have an hour or perhaps 45-minute classes. It can be tempting to avoid the warm-up because you want to get to the heart of the workout, you want to get to the meat, but that appetizer of the warm-up is what makes the meal of training so much more appetizing.

When I consider warm-ups, I see four parts to make them effective: low-risk cardio, joint mobility, intensifying cardio, and flexibility. Let's talk about what each one of those means.

Low-risk cardio is a simple, steady-state movement that allows you to get your heart rate up. It can be very individual. It could be jumping jacks for some people, but it could be pushups, it could be squats, or it could be a jog. It's anything that you can do without warming up and risking injury. It shouldn't be intense. It shouldn't do anything other than get your heart rate up 20, 30, 40 beats a minute. It shouldn't be something that makes you sweat. It shouldn't be difficult, and if you can't continually talk at a normal rate through it, it's too much. This first phase is important because it allows your body to recognize that it is about to receive something more intense, that you're going to start exercising. Your body doesn't know that it's martial arts versus weight training versus running. Your body just knows, "Hey, I'm going to do something more intense soon," and it prepares for it.

The second part, joint mobility, allows you to manipulate all your joints in full ranges of motion, or as full a range of motion as you can without being risky to your joints or your body. It's a lot of circles, focus on moving your joints, from the head down to the toe. Take a few seconds for a few revolutions, or a few hinges at each joint, and check-in with your body. What hurts? What feels better after you move it? The two things needed for healthy joints are compression and movement. We're getting the movement here.

The third step, intensifying cardio, could be any of those things that you did in that first low-risk cardio stage but at a higher rate. You should be able to talk through this, but not have a conversation. Your words should come sporadically. You should have to focus on what you're doing, and it should be challenging. This stage does not need to be extremely challenging. In the low-risk cardio stage, maybe you're running a 15-minute mile, and maybe in this stage you're at 8-, 10-, 12-minutes, something faster, something that requires effort.

The final stage, flexibility, is very important to us as martial artists, and something that a lot of schools pride themselves on, but flexibility requires being warm. If you stretch a tight muscle, you increase the risk of injury. It is unlikely that most of us get many benefits out of stretching cold muscles because we can't relax into them in the way that we can when we're warm. Stretching shouldn't hurt, but it should be uncomfortable. There's a big difference between pain and discomfort, and if you can read this book, you probably know the difference.

How long should a warm-up take? Five to fifteen minutes is all you need. The more focused you are, the more diligent you are with what you're doing, building a routine that works for you, the faster it can be. At no point during your warm-up should you really cool off. If you're doing a longer warm-up, you may have to revisit the low-risk cardio stage, that low-intensity round of pushups, squats, or jogging, in between the other phases because you need to keep that heart rate up a little bit.

If you have a particularly difficult training session, you might want to do some of your warm-up movements as a cool down, to spend 5 minutes relaxing, stretching, bringing your heart rate back down, rather than dashing off the training floor, throwing on your shoes, and getting in the car. It can help shuttle waste fluid and waste products that your body generates as you're doing something intense. It can help move those around to the organs responsible for processing them in a much more effective way rather than letting them just hang out. What does that mean for you? It can mean less soreness and faster progress when we think about the adaptations your body takes on when you're training.

The Importance of Muscle Memory

People throw around the term "muscle memory" quite a bit, but really, it's not the muscles that are remembering anything. Muscles are dumb. They don't know anything. They do what we tell them to do, but what's telling the muscles what to do? It's your brain, and specifically when we talk about "muscle memory," we're talking about your central nervous system.

We're all familiar with the idea of, and even the practice of getting better at certain things when we do them repeatedly. When we practice a thing, it becomes easier to do, it becomes more ingrained in us, and when we talk about it from a martial arts perspective, we talk about being able to apply techniques quickly and efficiently without thinking about them.

When we talk about training movements over and over again, we think of them in terms of muscle memory, but it's the central nervous system that is conditioned to apply those techniques properly and at the proper time by thickening the myelin, the pathways in the brain. As we practice those movements, the pathways get thicker, it gets easier to transmit a signal requesting a certain movement for a certain stimulus, and our hand goes out, or our foot goes out to apply the technique.

If you've never experienced the joy of executing the right technique at the right time without having to think anything about it, you're missing out. Keep training and you'll get there. For the rest of you who have, you know how special it is. It makes you feel like your training is now validated. Everything that you've worked for can be applied.

But there is a downside to becoming that conditioned. You can become predictable, and many of us when we reach those middle to upper-middle ranks - say blue, green, brown belt - we become predictable to fighters who have been around a while. Sure, our movements work well when we're sparring against someone of equal or lower rank, but when we rely on a small set of techniques that our body has been conditioned to apply, it's easy to spot what we're doing. It can also mean that you're going to respond improperly given a certain technique if the person you're sparring with gets you to think it's something else, or maybe more accurately, gets you to react as if it's something else.

The better we get at that certain core set of movements that we use properly and well and feel good about, the less diversity we're going to have, and the less likely we are to practice other movements because, hey, this small set of movements works. Nothing is stopping you from building a larger and larger toolbox of movements to refer to, whether it's conscious or unconscious. When we talk about muscle memory, sure, build up a core of a few techniques, but don't stop adding to that pile of movements that you can dig into. Routine is the enemy. Practicing your movements in different ways, at different speeds, different power levels, different angles, different stances, all enhance not only "muscle memory" - if we're going to continue calling it that - but your ability to enjoy your training and your ability to execute your techniques in the proper way when the time calls for it.

Practicing a front kick 10,000 times is wonderful, but if you always practice it at the exact same height, what happens when you spar someone taller or shorter? What happens when you need to put that kick in a different place? By practicing it 10,000 times, you have told your body, "This is where a front kick goes," but if you start to vary it, if you start to connect the stimulus of observing an open spot on a person's body with executing that kick, you can get better at automatically making sure that foot seeks out that target without even thinking about it.

Being aware and conscious of what you're doing and how you're doing it is very important but having a fundamental set of movements that you can use that you don't need to think about is an important part of your martial arts training.

Getting Stronger

When we talk about strength, it is easy to see the value. No matter what it is you are looking to do, whether it's martial arts or life in general, being stronger has its advantages. In fact, there's nothing that you can do that isn't made better, easier, or improved by getting stronger. Sure, you may say that as you get stronger you lose flexibility, but that's not necessarily true, and there is science to back that up. As martial artists, the stronger we are, the more effective we are, especially when we consider things from the perspective of self-defense. Stronger people are, to be direct, harder to kill. Your blocks, your strikes, and your kicks are all more effective when you can apply more strength behind them.

The way that people get stronger is through resistance training. Whether it is weight training or calisthenics using your body weight, there are several ways that you can get stronger, but they all require using resistance against gravity. I could write an entire book on how to get stronger, and maybe someday I will, but when we talk about developing strength, the ways that are most effective for us as martial artists tend to involve what are called compound movements. Those are movements that utilize multiple joints at a time. Think about a squat. Not only does it correlate well with a lot of our stances, but a squat also uses multiple joints. Thus, it's more applicable when we go to kick or step because we've gotten stronger through those multi-joint patterns versus simply doing a bicep curl.

One thing that is not often discussed in martial arts is the importance of strengthening connective tissue. Sure, we want to get stronger in our muscles, and maybe we even want to grow our muscles for aesthetics, but as we get stronger and we start applying significant force, that can take a toll on our connective tissue, our joints, ligaments, things like that. When you look at the development programs of gymnastics, young gymnasts spend a tremendous amount of time getting stronger, especially through their joints, through their connective tissue. As we become more effective martial artists, and we can strike faster and harder, joints must be able to handle the strain, or else you can develop injuries.

Once someone understands the importance of becoming stronger, they'll generally ask, "How often should I work on developing this strength?" Ideally, do it as much as you have time for, so long as it doesn't hinder your general martial arts training or other important aspects of your life. You can work on this stuff every day. That doesn't mean you should spend four hours a day in the gym seven days a week, very few people's bodies can handle that, but it does mean that doing a few sets of pushups two or three times a day can be effective. In fact, frequency is the number one determinant of adaptation, whether we are talking about adaptation of strength, or flexibility, or any of the other things we talk about in this book. The more often you work on them, the better you'll get, and the faster you'll see results.

Of course, any amount is better than nothing. One day a week is better than zero, five minutes is better than none, and how much you work on this in your martial arts classes determines how often you should be working on it outside of class. You can train at home, you can train at the gym, or you can hire a trainer. If you're working at home, tools like kettlebells or dumbbells, maybe a balance board can be effective in developing strength and generalized fitness that you can bring back into your martial arts training, and you can do so for a relatively low cost. Of course, if it's something that you're serious about, you probably want to get a gym membership or invest in much larger complement of equipment.

When we talk about strength, quite often, people confuse strength and power. Let's include the idea of speed so we can talk about power and strength appropriately. Power is a combination of strength and speed. Speed and strength are very different things. Let's think about them in terms of a pushup. Everyone understands what a pushup is. When we think about pushups done for speed, you're doing pushups as quickly as you can. When you think about strength pushups, you might do the same pushup with a weight or person sitting on your back, but when you do powerful pushups - and this is what we care most about as martial artists - you do pushups so hard and so fast that your hands pop up off the ground at the top. It is those powerful movements that make what we do effective.

You can be the strongest person in the world, but if your techniques are slow, not only will they never land on their target, but it won't hurt. You can be the fastest person in the world, but if there's no muscle, no strength behind the techniques, you'll be good at point sparring, and that's about it. However, if you are powerful, if you're able to apply both strength and speed through a variety of angles and types of motion, you will become a very effective martial artist who can hold their own in a wide variety of situations.

Strength is important not only to every martial artist, but every human being, and it's something that I would like to see included more prominently in martial arts classes. Whether it's pushups or squats, or even deep statically-held - in other words, unmoving - stances, there are a lot of ways you can develop strength within the context of martial arts. The stronger we get, the better we get in and out of our training.

Aging

Aging is inevitable. No one has found a way to stop it. We can slow it down, we can age gracefully, we can even become better as we age depending on how you apply your efforts, but it is going to happen.

When we think about aging in the martial arts, we are talking about both physical and mental changes, and those changes occur slowly over time. Fortunately, martial arts are one of those pursuits that, as the physical body starts to deteriorate, our mental acuity, or at least our experience, allows us to progress in other ways. We can become more patient, and we can become humble, as we develop skills that aren't necessarily physical.

When you start to look at the way people age, we see that some of the number one determinants of people being able to age in their own home under their own care have to do with using skills that they don't use all the time. Reaching into overhead cabinets, the ability to stand up on your own, climb stairs, these are all things that we take for granted in our younger years, but as we get older, some people decide that they're not able to do them. They're not willing to put in the effort. This may sound callous, but that's not my intention. Every one of us can maintain a high level of physical health as we age, but it requires more effort, and it requires a certain mindset. I've watched people age amazingly well, in and out of martial arts, but the martial artists that I've seen age the best are those who continue to go to class and who defy the number that is associated with their age. Yes, their birth certificate may say that they're 65, 75, even 85 years old, but they laugh in class, they're happy to partner up with younger students, and they do what they can when they can, which, let's be honest, that's what all of us should be doing.

What should you not do as you age? You should not stop doing anything that you still have the capacity to do. If you stop doing something, you will lose the ability to do it eventually. You should not stop going to class. You should not stop your training. Training is important, and if you want to be a healthy, well-rounded martial artist and person as you get older, going to class, engaging in these social activities, and showing the younger folk that you can still hang is important. You should not stop sparring either. Maybe you change the parameters, maybe you change the speed at which you operate, and maybe you have to find different training partners, but I've known some utterly incredible martial artists who outside of martial arts training, one would assume from the way they look or from their age that they were completely incapable of operating at such a high physical level.

The body does start to change as we get older, and there are things that must adjust, but there's a difference between stopping things and delaying things. If you're injured, you may have to delay certain kinds of training, but you never have to stop them. The muscles that you do not use, the techniques you do not practice, will degrade, and you'll lose access to them.

The very best martial artists find ways to continue to get better, even if that doesn't mean physical growth. When you are in your 60s, 70s, and 80s, you're probably not pulling off new advanced kicking combinations that you were unable to do in your 20s, 30s, and 40s. You can, however, be more of a student of history, you can understand the way the body works, and you can observe using the context of your experience to better understand not only the human body but martial arts and people in general.

We went over the things you shouldn't do. What *should* you do? You should do things that set you up for success. All the things that make you healthy when you are younger make you healthy when you are older. Getting enough sleep, eating good food, drinking good water, getting physical activity, these are all things that will help your body maintain what it has. Resistance training becomes even more critical as we age as it increases bone density, or if not increases it, maintains it. Sleep is where we recover. It is the place where your body heals the most effectively. Getting enough sleep as well as getting good quality sleep becomes critical.

If you think something is off, don't be afraid to have blood work done. Find a good doctor who will allow you to age in the way that you want to age. If your doctor says, "Oh, it's just because you're older," don't take that. That's an unacceptable answer, and there are plenty of doctors out there who will work with you to make sure that you are living the life that you want to live under your terms.

Flexibility is something that tends to get lost as we age, and that is often because of a lack of movement and a lack of diverse movement, which martial arts helps us maintain. Developing your own routine, addressing your weaknesses as you age, regardless of what age you are now, is important. If you are 20, set yourself up to be a healthy 80-, 90-, 120-year-old, whatever it is you want to be. If the things you are doing now aren't going to help you get there later, then consider revising those decisions.

I'm not embarrassed to say that I've had multiple people in their 60s take me to task sparring, even when I've tried as much as I can. This has occurred at a variety of ages over my training career. Now, at 40, there are plenty of people in their 20s that I can still show new things. I can honestly say that I'm in the best shape of my life because of the way I approach my day and my training. I'm stronger, I'm more flexible, and a lot of that is because I work smarter at the things that matter. I get better sleep, I have more movement, and probably most importantly I have a better outlook on life and on my training.

Flexibility

When we talk about flexibility in the martial arts, there are several things that come to mind. We think about people kicking really high or doing interesting jump-spin combinations that seem to defy their hip being in the socket at all, but flexibility is imperative, not just to martial arts training but to life in general. So is mobility, but there are differences between flexibility and mobility. What are they?

Flexibility is the ability of something to bend without breaking. It's you touching your toes. It's you being able to kick overhead. It doesn't necessarily mean you're able to hold those positions for a long time, or even to be able to do them simply or easily. Mobility is the ability to do those things easily. The ability to walk and have all your joints that are involved in that process move without pain, that's mobility.

As human beings, we can be flexible without being mobile, and we can be mobile without being flexible. Most people have a certain amount of mobility, but they don't have a lot of flexibility. Flexibility could also be thought of as using the end range of motion. I might be able to kick to the waist easily, that's mobility, but to be able to kick over my head, that's flexibility.

Of course, as martial artists, we want both, and we want to work on both as often as we can, because with frequency comes the adaptation, the ability for the body to incorporate these new ranges of motion and make them part of our training in our lives.

As we have said often in this book and on the show, a diverse martial artist is a better martial artist. The more range of motion you have, the more angles and ways you can manipulate your body, the better a martial artist you are. It gives you more options for how to train or fight or defend yourself, or simply play with the motion of martial arts.

If you want to improve your mobility, you can do that while you have cold muscles. It is possible, and it's okay because you're not pushing the range of motion beyond anything safe. You move your joints within the full range of motion of what you're able to do without feeling strain or stress pushing back against you. This should be part of your warmup, using your joints to a full range of motion, for example, walking. The body is designed to do a lot of walking. Most of us don't think of walking as doing anything particularly strenuous unless you're doing it for long distances. If you think of some older folks who have lost the ability to walk, that's what we are hoping to prevent. Working your mobility is maintaining range of motion and even increasing it through joint manipulation and just general use of the body. To say it another way, if you don't use it, you lose it. Identifying all the different ways that you can move your body and using those periodically, even daily, is critical.

When we talk about stretching or flexibility, we're talking about something a little more intensive, something that requires a bit more work. You DON'T want to stretch with cold muscles. Not only is it counterproductive, but it can also cause serious injury. Stretching done properly can convince your body that a new range of motion is actually safe, and you can start to incorporate that into your daily routines and practices and start to see additional angles and movement that you can go through.

The best progress in flexibility comes when you can relax as many of the muscles involved as possible. The more muscles you have fighting against you trying to stretch into a particular posture, the less likely it's going to be a permanent adaptation. Let's take the center split as an example. Most people practice the center split with their feet on the ground widening their legs, and that forces them to use muscles to hold themselves up. That can work, and plenty of people have developed greater flexibility in that way using this posture. My preference, and the way I recommend doing this - and again, I'm not a doctor, I have to preface everything I say with that - imagine that you lay on your back, slide your butt up against a wall, put your legs straight up against the wall so now your bent at 90 degrees, and let your legs fall open, slowly. You can control them with your arms if need be, but now you're achieving the same posture without having to fight to stay up. You can relax into it over time. This, based on my experience and my research, is a much more effective way to build flexibility over time.

Keep in mind that stretching should never hurt. If it hurts, if it's painful, if it's anything more than uncomfortable, you're risking injury. What is it that allows you to stretch? What is it that allows you to incorporate new movement and hold onto that new movement? It's your body's central nervous system recognizing that motion as safe. The more you have to fight to get into that position, the less convincing your signal to the central nervous system will be. That's where frequency and small progress, incremental adaptation, becomes important.

When we talk about stretching, there are two main kinds of stretching. We have dynamic stretching and static stretching. The examples we just gave with the center split, those are static stretches. You're holding a posture, trying to relax into it. Dynamic stretching involves moving toward the end range of motion in the hope that the nervous system, muscles, and everything involved will relax and allow incremental progress. It doesn't necessarily mean that the progress is maintained over time, but it usually can be if done effectively. What's an example of stretching those same muscles dynamically? Standing in a side fighting stance and swinging your leg up in what many people call a leg raise or a leg rise stretch. I use both types, and most of my flexibility training involves static stretching, but I prefer dynamic stretching. I find it to be far simpler, I find it to be safer, and it can be incorporated as part of a warmup. There is certainly benefit to both, and a good stretching routine will have both in it.

I have found that the best resource in understanding what muscles are tight and which ones to work on through my flexibility training is a good massage therapist, someone who understands the body well enough and can help you work through ranges of motion and identify what stretches will help isolate certain muscles. That's not to say that you cannot make a lot of progress on your own. That's not to say that there aren't a tremendous number of resources out there. Several of the guests that we've had on Martial Arts Radio have their own books and videos on flexibility, and you should check them out. Flexibility is something that becomes even more important if you want to maintain or even increase your mobility as you age.

The Paradox of Overweight Martial Artists

If we want the rest of the world to see martial artists as athletes and as individuals who can help keep us healthy and in shape, we must address this seeming paradox of overweight martial artists. There are quite a few overweight martial artists, probably roughly the same as the general population in proportion. The last numbers I saw said that about 60% of the United States was overweight. Based on what I have seen attending martial arts competitions and traveling around, it seems roughly the same. Maybe it is a bit better, say maybe 50% of martial artists are overweight, but it's certainly not any dramatic shift such that the rest of the world will look and say, "Ah, martial artists are all in really good shape."

Why is that a problem? If we are telling the world that martial arts are great for fitness and health, and we have a lot of martial artists who are overweight, including and even especially instructors, we're counterproductive. We're confusing the rest of the world. We say, "Hey, martial arts are good for fitness," but we're not very fit. That doesn't make sense. In fact, it makes everything we say suspect. It makes people doubt our integrity, the genuineness of what we're saying, the truth.

I do not mean to disparage anyone. Being fit, being healthy is challenging. I have my own struggles with it. I'm not saying that the people who are overweight aren't facing their own battles, but I am saying that we need to decide. If we are going to tell the world that martial arts are great for fitness, we need to hold ourselves accountable and stop promoting unhealthy, overweight people to positions of authority, or we can stop telling the world that martial arts are great for fitness.

Bringing this up may sound callous or disrespectful, and that's not how I mean it. I am looking at this from the perspective of what is best for the martial arts, and what is best for you as a martial artist. If you're looking to train to be healthy and fit, you probably don't want to train under people who are not fit and not healthy themselves. This may be something that you look for in a martial arts school. I've trained under people who are overweight, I've trained under people who are not, and the classes, the way they are run, and the types of drills that we do are different. There is certainly an impact on the way you train as it applies to your fitness.

We can say that a lot of higher-ranking martial artists are spending more of their time teaching than they are training, and this can be part of why we see a lot of higher-ranking martial artists becoming overweight, but is that the only reason? I don't know. I am not a high-ranking martial artist. I am not an overweight martial artist, so I can't speak, even from my own personal experience, but I can say that if we are going to tell people that martial arts makes you fit and healthy and better able to withstand the rigors and the challenges of being attacked, we need to make sure that the people who are promoting and teaching these things are not counter-examples themselves.

There are only so many ways the human body can move, and only a portion of them make sense through the lens of combat. Thus, there is more that we have binding us as martial artists than dividing us.

Part 4 – Getting Help

Speaking with Your Instructor

If you spend much time in the martial arts, inevitably at some point, you are going to need to bring an issue to your instructor. That can be intimidating. It can be downright scary to talk to your instructor and voice a need, or even more terrifying, a problem, an issue you're having in class. Maybe it's the way they're doing something, or the way one of the senior students is doing something. As scary as it is, it is imperative that you voice your concerns to your instructor. One of two things is going to happen when you do that. In the first case, you are going to be heard, you are going to feel good about your experience, and it's going to reinforce the fact that you belong there in that school. On the flip side, if you're not heard, if you're not feeling good about the exchange, if you don't feel like the instructor cares, maybe you decide it's time to look for another school.

Martial artists are expected to be and generally are good people. When someone crosses the line, when someone does something that they shouldn't have done, there's usually punishment. It's not necessarily formal, and it's not quite the same as being in elementary school or going to prison, but we do tend to take care of our own, and we also tend to punish our own, whether it's speaking with someone who crosses the line, or possibly all the way up to removing someone from the school. Sometimes, in between, there is physical discipline, and I think you know what I mean by that.

Many martial arts schools focus on and prioritize improving the character of the students in attendance. We talk a lot about this with children. We don't talk about it in the same way with adults, but it happens. People who come to martial arts classes tend to progress as human beings, they become better people, and it's something that we value in the martial arts, but that doesn't always mean that everyone that is training is doing so for the right reasons or makes it a priority to take care of those around them. If something pops up with someone that you're training with, it's important to speak about it with your instructor.

Conversations with your instructor could also be quite personal. Let's talk about the most innocuous thing that you would want to bring to your instructor - a personal injury. If you walk into class and you're banged up, you fell, you're hurt, but you still want to train, talking to your instructor and saying, "Hey, this is what's going on with me, but I still want to be here," that lets them know that maybe the standards that they're going to hold you to that day on certain movements shouldn't be as high. Maybe your knee isn't functioning right, so your stances won't be as low. That's okay, and you should never be afraid to speak to your instructor about that.

By the same token, let them know about a planned absence. That's something else that should come up, because if you've never been an instructor, you may not know that if you build a format for 25 people and 15 show up, it might completely throw off the lesson plan. Knowing who is going to show up, at least having a rough idea, can be helpful. Don't be afraid to let your instructor know, be it in-person at a prior class, in an email, or some other method that your instructor might prefer.

There are other times where you'll want to speak to your instructor, and some of these might be a little more challenging. What if there's someone in class that you feel is disrespectful to you, is intentionally harming you, or maybe even not intentionally, but you can't seem to find a way to work with this student in a way that doesn't hurt? I've trained with a number of these people, and it stinks. Enlisting the assistance of an instructor, whether that's for disciplinary reasons, or even just to seek advice, can be helpful because sometimes you don't know the reasons for certain behaviors. Maybe there's something more going on. Maybe there's something you're doing, or you could be doing differently that could change the outcome.

As intimidating as it can be to speak to your instructor, inevitably we're all going to deal with issues in our training, and the decision whether to speak to an instructor hinges on one thing. Have you done your best to handle the situation in a respectful, empathetic, and understanding manner? If that is something that you can do, that should be done first. if it's not something that you're able to do, if it's something that you're uncomfortable doing, maybe you're fearing backlash in having a conversation with someone, maybe you're a new student and there's a senior student who you think picks on you - as much as it stinks, that does happen - going to an instructor may make more sense. It may also make more sense to speak to a different senior student if the issue is with a senior student, or just, in general, to speak to a senior student to get advice before you speak to the instructor, working your way up the chain as it were, because every school has its own culture. Every school has this way that they do things, and some things are appropriate to bring to your instructor, some things are not, and if you're nervous, you're probably going to be less nervous speaking to someone who is not the instructor, someone who has been there for a while and has more knowledge of what to do than you do, and that's okay.

No matter who you are, where you are training, what the issue is, or who you speak with, it is never acceptable, if you bring the issue up respectfully, to be treated poorly for bringing it up. Let me give you an example. In most martial arts schools, it is considered bad form to ask when you would be testing for your next rank. Not all, but most. As someone who has been training for a while, I would never go to my instructor and say, "Hey, I think I'm ready for my next rank. When do I get to test?" That wouldn't come across well. If I'm training at a new school, I may go to a senior student or even the instructor and ask the question, "Hey, I don't want to overstep any boundaries, but I am curious about the way testing for rank is handled in your school. I've trained at several different schools. It's handled differently at different places, and I want to make sure that I am holding to the standards and expectations in this school regarding rank and testing." If you approach it in that way, it is unlikely you're going to be treated disrespectfully or shunned.

Any issue that you may have, you can approach that from either a respectful and questioning way, the way a student should always ask a question, or with confidence and arrogance and get shut down. In the end, don't be afraid to ask questions because that's how we learn.

Taking a Break from Training

One of the most divisive, even frustrating and anger-inducing questions that comes up in the martial arts is the idea around taking a break. To some, the idea that you would ever want to stop training temporarily is mind-blowing, something that they could never imagine for themselves. For others, martial arts are something that they do intermittently. It's something that they fit into their life around other things. It isn't the priority, and guess what? It is okay to look at martial arts differently. It's okay to train for ten years and then stop for a few and then start training again. It's okay to train six months out of the year, and then take a break the other six. Martial arts will always be there for you when you're ready for it. It's okay that we understand that. Not everyone agrees, and not every instructor feels the same way, especially when that instructor's livelihood rests on your attendance at class. Let's face it, martial arts aren't for everyone, and every martial arts school isn't appropriate for every martial artist, so forcing people into training continually, or stopping entirely, is a very silly, black-and-white binary standard. To say that taking a break is wrong is silly.

Taking a break is not a good solution for being bored. If you're bored, there's a good chance that boredom comes from the way you are approaching your training. To say it another way, it might be, and I would say it probably is your fault. You can put something different into your training, and that can make it less boring. It can make it new and exciting. You can approach your training with all sorts of different mindsets. I've had great classes and terrible classes that were essentially the same. Same people, same instructor, same material, same drills, same time of year, even the same uniform, but what was different was my expectation for myself and for my training that day.

The times that I recommend taking a break are the same times that I have taken a break myself - when I find myself losing passion, when there's so much going on in my life that my martial arts training, especially attending a particular class or classes, is no longer a refuge from my life but instead adds responsibility, adds weight to my shoulders. I love martial arts, and I never want to see it as a burden, nor do I want anyone else to see it in that way. People don't do well when they're forced to do things, even when that force is coming internally. Forcing children to go to martial arts doesn't usually work out well, because as soon as they're old enough or have a good excuse, they stop training, and there's a good chance that they will never go back to it.

If you are going to take a break, there are a few things that you should do to get the most out of it. You should have a defined endpoint. "I'm going to take a month off." "I'm going to take these two weeks off." "I'm going to take the next three months off." It depends on why you are taking a break as to what an appropriate amount of time will be.

You should tell your instructor about it. They may try to talk you out of it. That's part of their job. Their job is to get the best out of you. They're a coach, in a sense, and if you're not on the field, they can't help you. If you fully understand why you're taking a break if you feel confident this is a good move for you, and you go to them and say, "I'm going to take the next month off — just a month. I will be back on this date. I'm losing my passion for my training," or, "I have a variety of family commitments coming up,

81

and I can't dedicate my emotional energy and my physical energy to training right now in a way that works well for me," they don't have to agree with it. It's your decision.

If they don't respect your decision, that's okay. Sometimes you have to agree to disagree. If they're not willing to accept that, again, as we've said in other sections of this book, maybe you need a different school. While a martial arts instructor probably knows better than you what you need in terms of martial arts training, they don't know better than you what you need in life. Only you know that.

If you are an instructor and someone comes to you, and they want to take a break, don't argue with them. Understand them. Help them work through whatever it is and be supportive. If you have a family atmosphere, if you truly represent yourself and your school as being supportive and helping people through their lives and getting better at the martial arts, this is something that you need to learn how to do. Don't argue with them. Give them suggestions. Give them ideas on how to maximize the impact of taking a break.

If you are someone that operates a school where you charge tuition ahead every month, maybe you work into your policy that you defer out. Some schools will continue to charge but find a way to make sure that people aren't paying for nothing. There are a bunch of different ways that you can slice that, and I'm not going to go into those here.

When someone is on a break, make sure that they don't stop hearing from you. Send them an email every week or two. Call them. Ask how they're doing. Make sure that they know that it's out of support, and not simply to find out when they're coming back to class. If someone leaves for family-related stuff, check-in with them. Can you be helpful? Can the other people in the school be helpful? Remember, the friendlier the atmosphere, the more your martial arts school has a culture around a social aspect, where people are friends in and out of training, the more they know they have a group who values and supports them, the less often someone will take a break, and the less often someone will leave entirely. If that's not something you have integrated into your school, maybe it's time to look at how to do that.

The better you get at martial arts,
the more you discover there is to learn.

Part 5 – Martial Arts Culture

The Importance of Martial Arts in Popular Culture

Culture has always been an important part of martial arts. It's not uncommon for martial artists to trade their favorite movies and books back and forth, or to argue over who the better actors were. There's a social aspect to martial arts movies and television that I don't see in other sports or pursuits. It's so strongly tied to what we do that there are movies that can have dramatic influence on how martial arts are trained and who decides to do it.

The generally accepted first martial arts film was *Billy Jack*. With the starring role and quite a bit of the behind-the-scenes work, Tom Laughlin was the first true big martial arts actor that many people saw. Tom Laughlin's Hapkido instructor, Master Bong Soo Han, who some consider the father of Hapkido in the United States, played the sheriff role. We've had several guests mention that *Billy Jack* is one of their favorites, if not their favorite martial arts film of all time. If you've seen it, you know it's cheesy. It's odd, the combat isn't anything stellar, but like many beloved martial arts movies, there's a special quality to it, something that just kind of sticks with you. It makes you want to be that hero that shows up, the one who uses martial arts to help people. At the time the movie was filmed, there was absolutely nothing like it, and it earned over $60 million when it was released in 1973. It even surpassed other movies that we often think of as being much better from the modern era, like *Hero* and *The Forbidden Kingdom*. In fact, adjusted for inflation, at the time of this recording, it's the 53rd highest-grossing film of all time. It only cost $800,000 to make.

The next big movie that is mentioned all the time on our show is, of course, is *Enter the Dragon*. Part of the reason for that is that it launched the careers of several prominent martial artists. Jackie Chan, Sammo Hung, Pat Johnson, they were all involved in that movie. It had a slightly larger budget than *Billy Jack*, just over $800,000, and it grossed $90 million globally. It, too, has cheesy elements. The fight scenes are below what we would consider standard for today's movies, but there's a magical quality about it, and the best martial arts movies, books, TV shows, even the best martial artists, seem to have an almost magical, mystical quality to what they do. Other movies have had just as strong if not a stronger impact like *The Karate Kid*, or the original *Teenage Mutant Ninja Turtles*. Will we look back on movies like *John Wick* or *The Raid*, which are held in high regard today, in the same way later? Maybe.

Because martial arts aren't something that is practiced by everyone, it's difficult for those of us who train to step out into the world and feel like what we do is broadly valued. When we see a mass-market movie or television show or pick up a book, it validates what we do. It reminds us that the rest of the world, even if they don't train in or understand what we do, on some level many of them appreciate what we do. That can make it easier to invest your time or your money into a pursuit that gets cocked eyebrows from the people around us.

Where Have the Martial Arts Heroes Gone?

When people think about heroes in the martial arts, they tend to think about celebrities, and I guess that makes sense. Heroes tend to be larger than life. They're people we look up to, people who have done big, dramatic things.

When we think about heroes in the context of martial arts, we don't have a lot from which to choose. People tend to think about movie stars or those who have had competitive success. That's not to say that martial arts instructors or those running non-profit organizations that benefit children, that these people aren't heroes, but these aren't the types of folks, the types of martial artists that teenagers are putting up on their walls. As trivial as it may seem, we need people that are worthy of going on posters on teenagers' walls.

One of the things that allows people to continue working on something that is difficult and has no endpoint is role models. While martial arts instructors and people that show up at the local tournaments and dominate the field are people to look up to, they are attainable. Those are people that we could all see ourselves becoming. While that's a good thing, it's also a bad thing that we don't have others, people that we could never in our wildest dreams become.

It wouldn't matter how hard I played basketball and practiced. I would never have become anything on the caliber of an NBA player. You could say the same about any professional sport. I wasn't built for that. That wasn't my path, no matter how much at points in my life I wanted it to be. It's important to have people to look up to that we could all become and people that, no matter how hard we try, we will never become. This is part of why I think Bruce Lee continues to be our biggest celebrity, our biggest hero. He did some utterly remarkable things, and he died young, and that's a recipe for greatness. Bruce Lee has been canonized as great, as above all the rest of us, and while there may be some truth to that, there are also plenty of stories that we've heard on Martial Arts Radio, and stories that I've read elsewhere, that say that while he was an exceptional martial artist, he was just a man.

When we talk about those who have achieved amazing things competitively, we tend to be talking about those who competed in the 60s, the 70s, or the 80s, when competition was a little more focused, when you had fewer competitions, more competitors, and the victories meant a little bit more. I don't know how we get martial arts heroes, truly larger-than-life people that will go on posters on walls, but I believe that we need them, and we need to find a way as an industry to cultivate them, because it will mean a path forward for all of us, something to aspire to, and that will keep people training and keep people working hard to become the next whoever-that-is.

*Martial Arts is always there for you
when you're ready to train.*

Part 6 – Competition

Overview

Competition is a substantial and important part of the martial arts. Maybe it's because martial arts have their roots in military and self-defense on the battlefield, or maybe just because it's human nature to want to test your skills against others. Either way, when we think of martial arts, quite often we think of martial arts competition, of sparring, or of performing forms in front of others for judgement. It's something that, if not most, many martial artists have participated in, and it's an important part of our culture.

I have no numbers to back this up, but I would venture that most martial artists participate in at least one competition at some point during their martial arts career, and in fact, there are martial arts schools that focus on competitions, that all of their training is based on competing and succeeding in that environment. When we think about the skills learned in competitions, they're excellent skills. They're things that we all want to get better at, or at least should: the ability to perform in front of strangers, the ability to face your fears when you're competing against people that you don't know, maybe people that you believe to be better than yourself. On top of that, competing can teach you a tremendous amount about who you are, how you practice, and how you see yourself.

The most common style of competition is referred to as open competition, and these competitions vary. They can be very small, they can be massive, some of them have different rules, but the general idea is you can participate, as long as you follow the rules, regardless of the style that you practice. Of course, there are also closed tournaments where you have to participate in a certain style or perhaps a certain organization to even be eligible for entry and participation.

Forms competition varies dramatically, not only between open and closed tournaments but even among open tournaments. Different rule sets, different emphasis on certain elements, leave people not only impressed but also sometimes upset. The first-place form at one event might not even place, might be dead last in another event. I've seen it happen.

These days there are a tremendous number of martial arts competitions, ranging from very large, very professionally run events, to very small, even within the martial arts school itself. I'm a firm believer that competition is a good thing, not necessarily for everyone but for the industry, and the more we can improve martial arts competitions, the more we can improve the martial arts. The more exciting we can make these events, the more we can attract outside interest, outside money, and that facilitates a lot of things, including paying martial arts competitors more when they are victorious.

If we want to make martial arts competitions more exciting, if we want to bring in more interest from people, whether they are or are not martial artists, there are two main things that we're looking at accomplishing. One, we're offering more events. Most martial arts competitions have forms, sparring, and maybe some kind of weapons forms. Yes, there are plenty of events that offer demonstration teams and split forms into traditional and creative and things of that nature, but those events aren't really that different. You know what's different? Breaking. I've watched breaking at events, and it's something that non-martial artists can relate to. How many pieces of wood did that person put their elbow through? More than that person? Then, they win. That makes sense to them, and it can be done in a very exciting way.

Secondly, martial arts events need to add elements outside of competition such as better food and better venues. They need to keep the crowd engaged when they're not actively watching the competition. If we think about turning martial arts events into a spectacle, something dramatic, something that carries excitement and energy the way that, say, a professional sports game might, where a team will host people at their stadium, that's a big deal. Obviously, martial arts competitions that are being held over a weekend at an event space aren't going to be able to do the same sort of things as a football stadium that's hosting 50,000 people, but I use that simply as an example of the direction that I think we should all be moving.

In 2016, whistlekick held a competition, and I learned a tremendous amount about that. I even wrote a book based on the results, *How Not to Hold a Martial Arts Competition*. It's available on Amazon, and there's a full course with templates and a whole bunch of other things available at whistlekick.com. We did some things well, and we also did some things not so very well, and that's why the title is what it is. The goal of that event was not to make money (which is good, because we didn't), but it was simply to illustrate that some things could be done differently. We've watched throughout the New England tournaments that we attend how some of the ideas that we implemented have taken hold at some of the other events. It's great to watch that, and I hope that some of the others will continue to elevate and try and test new ideas.

Martial arts competitions are a great way to help people find another aspect of martial arts in which to engage. The more great competitions, the more we will retain and attract people to martial arts training, which helps all of us grow and succeed.

Value of Competition

Now that we have discussed the value of competition, let's talk more in-depth on how it can be helpful to people. Most martial artists have participated in at least one competition, and that could be a very small competition within their school, or it can be some large international event, or any variation in between. Plenty of martial artists are pro-competition, and when asked why, they'll say things like it helps you meet new people, and it helps you refine your skills and expose yourself to new ideas and methods. Basically, it gives you more tools to draw from to develop yourself as a human being and as a martial artist. There are other martial artists who don't see competition in as positive a light. They feel that it dilutes the true spirit of the martial arts, that it can promote ego, and that it can be horrendously subjective. All those points, the pros *and* the cons, are in most cases, right. The question is, which of those things is most important to you?

Human beings are incredibly adaptive. We tend to understand and grow to work with the knowledge and skills we encounter. If we spend a lot of time competing, we tend to develop better results. We learn how to adapt our form to make the referees happier. We tend to develop the physical skills to present our form better. When it comes to the more combat aspects, we'll develop better cardiovascular fitness. We learn which techniques work well for us and which ones don't. We learn how to avoid and how to block. We become better at that skill of tournament sparring.

If we never compete, we'll never develop the skills necessary to be successful as a competitor. If most of our time is spent in competition and training for competition, we're going to lose some of the non-competitive benefits of martial arts. For example, competitive forms can vary from non-competitive forms. I know that when I compete, my forms are slightly different than when I'm practicing them "traditionally."

One of the major debates, when we talk about the value of competition, is around the practical application of martial arts. Some people will say that martial arts are meant to be self-defense or personal development only, and it has no place in competition. Then there are other people who don't care about the practical aspects of martial arts. They compete because it's fun. In the end, the important thing is that you figure out what you like or don't like for yourself.

I think everyone should try to compete, even if it's only once. You are going to learn something. Even if that something is that you don't like competing, there's value there. To practice in preparation for something with an endpoint, a date where something is riding on the line, I think there's a lot of benefit in that, and it's different from practicing for testing. To showcase your skills in competition against other people, especially from other schools and other styles, I think is amazing. It's something that I found very important to my development as a martial artist.

 If nothing else, traveling to and competing in martial arts competitions can help you make new friends. Let's face it, we all need more martial arts friends. The people that I learned from, the people that I trained with, even the people that were my referees, many of them are friends now, 25 years later, and they've been instrumental in helping whistlekick grow.

The Role of Money

Even though it's not something we think about often, not something we talk about much, money plays a really big role in martial arts competitions. To be honest, it's more the absence of money that plays a really big role. Martial arts are a passionate pursuit for most people. Very few people pursue martial arts because they think they're going to get rich. In fact, I don't know a single person who has ever told me they started martial arts or started teaching or any aspect of martial arts, because they thought it would make them rich. I do know quite a few people who have taken financial hits to teach or to otherwise further invest themselves in the martial arts. I'm one of them.

When we look at martial arts competitions, cash prizes are relatively small, and in most competitions, non-existent. There are lots of different reasons for this. The economics of most tournaments doesn't allow big cash prizes. Some promoters feel that by offering money it attracts a negative element to their competitions. There are a variety of good reasons to compete, and money, at least right now, isn't really one of them, but what if we did offer larger cash prizes in competition? Forget for a moment how we would do that, but what if we did? Said simply, larger cash prizes at most events, at least at the largest events, would have a huge and positive effect on the martial arts.

I don't think you have to look any further than mixed martial arts and CrossFit to see the impact of offering larger and larger cash rewards. Both sports - or pursuits or whatever you want to call them - have grown substantially, have garnered television time, and have seen the best in the world dedicate their lives not just to the pursuit but to the competition. We see athletes, and we see people with endorsement deals, people making real money. In martial arts, if the cash prizes increase, the best competitors are likely to do the same thing. They'll stick around. They'll develop competitive circuits. They'll have endorsement deals. We'll see people start to get into martial arts because not only do they love it, but they see the opportunity to make a good income. Beyond a good income, people see the opportunity for fame and riches, and while that may not be the goal for everyone, it's a pretty important part of growing any sport. While martial arts defy the traditional definition for a sport, it's probably the best label we can use for it.

I see the competitive martial arts landscape as a free market. The larger and more cash payouts available, the more competitors will be competing, the more attendance at those events, and that means more events, and that means more profits, and that means more opportunity for those of us in the martial arts world to attract money from outside the martial arts world. I think getting outside money is one of the most important things we can do.

As we start to bring in some outside money and admittedly make some format changes that would make what we do more television-friendly, we would start to see more TV time, which means more non-martial arts sponsorship. With that outside money, we see endorsement deals, and people making a substantial living, athlete-caliber salary. We need that. We need that money; we need that growth. Why? That type of growth attracts attention, and it gives aspiring martial artists, the heroes, the popular culture validation that people playing football and soccer and basketball have and have had for a very long time. It gives us our martial arts heroes that I think are so critical to the growth and persistence of this thing that we love so much.

Participation Awards

The idea of participation awards is counter to the ethos of the martial arts. When you award a trophy for 1st, 2nd, and 3rd place, and then declare everyone else 4th or 5th place, give them ribbons, and say, "Hey, great job! You showed up," we start to validate the showing up, not the effort, not the results, but simply the participation. Yes, while there are martial arts schools out there that promote rank based primarily on the amount of attendance rather than skill and progress, that's not the case for most martial arts schools. Most martial arts schools do a great job of correlating effort with results among the students. Then, we go to a lot of martial arts tournaments and we see the exact opposite.

Mere participation should not have an award. That does not mean you can't give out things. I've participated in many events that gave me a shirt, or a gift bag, but at no time did they say, "This is your 4th place t-shirt." People don't value the things that they receive. They value what they work for. They appreciate the things that they've earned the most. If you work for something and you earn that first-place trophy, that's great, but if you show up, you pay money, and you receive a trophy, you've simply paid for a trophy. That is very similar to the type of martial arts schools that so many of us are all over social media railing against, the idea that you pay for something and receive it without putting in any certain amount of effort.

We all know spoiled people, and most of us really dislike spoiled people, and yet participation awards do nothing more than encourage that behavior. If you are someone who puts on competitions, and you want to give out something to the participants, that's great. That's fine, but I'm asking you, please don't call it a trophy. Don't call it an award. Don't say they earned 5th place. Instead, give them a certificate of participation. Make sure it's different than the first, second, and third-place awards. Make sure everyone knows that there is a difference. Whatever the reasons you might want to give out a participation award, remember, the world doesn't do that. People don't get by in life simply by existing or merely participating. We inherently value effort, and more so results, and the sooner that we accept this, and the earlier that we help children understand this, the better it is for everyone.

Improving Competitive Events

If you have been to more than one martial arts event, you know that there are differences between them. Some events are better than others, and in fact, some are A LOT better than others, but there are ways to improve them. Let's talk about those ways that martial arts events could be improved.

Every event has a culture or a vibe, and if you don't intentionally create it, it will be created for you. If you have a vision for your event, and that vibe is part of it, you can make sure that you construct that event and bring in the right people to make sure that your vision is maintained. However, without the maintenance of a vision, the people who assemble will be the ones who create it. Since you are only one person, they are going to have the final say over how that event feels.

One of the easiest ways to figure out how to create a vibe for an event and make sure that you use that vibe to your advantage is to figure out what the niche is for your event. Maybe it's a competition that has the broadest number of events. Maybe it's a training seminar that offers an all-in-one fee that includes the training, room and board, meals, a t-shirt, things like that. When you figure out what makes your event better and different, you can make sure you create the proper environment for the benefit of those attending or who want to attend.

The number one way to improve any event year over year is to talk to the attendees. What did they like? What did they dislike? Find ways to get honest feedback from them. The more people you talk to, the better the picture you're going to get, and the more accurate information you'll be able to assemble. Surveys can work, but surveys tend to be skewed to the people who really love you and the people who really disliked the event, and that doesn't necessarily give you an honest picture of your event.

I encourage that people aim for changing 15% of what they have done every year, and here's my logic. If you are running a recurring event, and you've done it well enough that you are going to do it again, and that people want to attend again, find 15% of it to test out. If that 15% goes completely south, if everything about it is a disaster, you've still got an event that is 85% as good as what you had the year before. More than likely, you'll get at least half right out of the things that you test. Looking at this as a score on a test, that's about a 92% (it's actually 92 ½%), and that's pretty darn good. If you continually take this approach to iterate by testing new things and keeping what works every year, you're going to have an amazing event, and in a few years, a phenomenal event. This is how the best of the best do everything, not just martial arts events. The best people in the world, the best businesses, even the best athletes continually test and try new things, keeping what works. There's no reason why it won't work for you.

At the same time, don't get too wrapped up in the way you've always done things. Be willing to evolve. Sometimes evolution requires big steps. Occasionally, that 15% needs to be 30% or 40%. Times change, and if you don't change with them, you may be falling away, falling behind, and that's not what you want. People have certain expectations for the things they do, whether it's a competition, or training, or a summer camp, and if you don't provide those minimum expectations, they are not likely to participate. Remember, people get bored with the same thing over and over and over. If you don't find a balance between keeping what works and bringing in some change, you'll see people stop showing up.

Finally, at the end of the day, remember, you are serving your customers, whether they are your martial arts students or people you don't even know. If you go into it from the mindset of service to construct an event that is for them, not for lining your pockets, everything will go far better. The irony is that the best businesses, the best long-standing, viable, sustainable businesses, focus on the customer experience. By doing that, the money shows up, but if you focus only on the money, you tend to miss everything else.

If you want to go deeper on this subject, I wrote a book about it - *How Not to Hold a Martial Arts Competition* - and that book is available on Amazon.

The idea of participation awards is a paradox. An award is given when you do something exceptional. Participating, by definition, is the minimum you can do.

Part 7 – Rank

Overview

When it comes to martial arts, I don't think there's anything more controversial, more debate-inspiring, than discussions about rank. When we talk about martial arts rank, there are plenty of directions in which we can take it, but let's start in this section with an overview of some of the dos and the don'ts.

First off, there is no right or wrong way of handling the promotion of martial arts students. If what you do works for you and your school, or you as the student are fully accepting of the way things are done, and everyone is on the same page and knows what's happening, then it's fine. I have seen different martial arts schools promote based on meeting a certain skill set. I've seen them promote based on certain amounts of time, certain amounts of attendance, combinations of those, and in each case, it worked for most of the people. Not everyone is going to do well in every martial arts school, and part of that is the way promotions are handled, and that's okay. Every martial arts school should handle rank in the way that works for them, and that will attract and retain the students for which that works.

Numerous martial arts schools, maybe even most, charge belt fees. They charge for that testing, and that is perfectly fine, but I disagree with it, and here's why. I think it's a contradiction. When you ask someone to pay money, it is generally viewed as a negative. It is a punishment, it's a requirement, yet in martial arts we should be uplifting and celebrating the event that is a promotion. Shouldn't we take that wonderful thing and strip away any potential for negativity?

You can look at that and say, "Yeah, Jeremy, that makes sense, but what about the revenue that comes in? Many of these schools make a good amount of money with these rank tests." That's absolutely right, but if we look at the amount that comes in and we think of that across the year, and then we distribute the money back into the monthly fees, that's going to be another $5 to $10 a month based on the fees that I've seen. I've consulted with a lot of businesses over the years, martial arts and non-martial arts, service-based and product-based, and one of the things that I've found in the service-based businesses - which martial arts fits pretty closely with - is that an increase of $5 - $10 per month to provide a service rarely kicks anyone out the door. It may give some people an excuse if they were already looking to leave, but for the loyal people that are there, you are not going to see a change. What's more, if we average that out, that's probably going to be more revenue overall because it means that everyone is contributing every month whether they are meeting their standards for their rank testing.

As with anything, there are exceptions. Sometimes in some schools, their standards require bringing in certain higher rank martial artists to oversee or validate the test. That costs money, and sometimes budgeting that can be challenging. Having that fee but making sure everyone understands why that fee is there, can help alleviate the negativity that comes with asking people for more money.

It can be really challenging to know who is ready to test for promotion and who is not, and unfortunately it is entirely subjective. Even in the most rigorous schools with the most clearly laid out standards, whether someone is meeting that standard is quite often subjective, and that subjectivity can lead to using promotion as a motivational tool. An instructor may promote people who may be on the bubble, who have the ability but maybe not the drive to try their best. The hope is that by pushing them up to the next rank, they'll work a little harder and grow into the rank. That can happen, but it might also not happen, and it requires knowing the student and knowing the culture in your school if you're the person making that call. If you're the student, knowing yourself, knowing what's expected of you, and trusting the instructor is an important part of your training.

When we talk about people who are just clearly not ready, promoting them is a disservice. Sure, maybe it keeps them in the school a little bit longer, but what does that do to the way everyone sees your school, from inside and outside? If your standards are being compromised or entirely subjective between students, that can cause problems. I've watched schools torn apart from the inside because someone that the general student population thought was not ready for a promotion earned one, and it made them question everything about the school and the integrity of the instructors. Promotion must be handled very carefully, and if anything, I would ask people to err on the side of being conservative. Make sure that students have nailed their requirements. If you're a student, make sure there's no question that you know your forms and techniques and whatever else is expected of you. Let there be no doubt that you deserve that rank.

At many martial arts promotions there are evaluation forms, maybe some kind of checklist or notes that people who make the decision will write on. If those exist, they should be shared with the student, especially if it contains criticism of a student's performance or maybe even behavior in there. I've been a part of these testing boards, and I've seen these students time and time again fail to address the concerns that I write down about their technique, forms, etc. It's clearly laid out. They have a path on how to improve, and they chose not to work on those things. They chose to work on maybe the things they are best at, or they enjoy the most. Fortunately for them, I'm not the instructor at those schools.

I would also like us to consider the idea of changing the term of *failing*. Instead of referring to a martial arts rank promotion as a *promotion* or *test*, what if we change the word to an *evaluation* or *assessment*? The word test can bring a lot of anxiety to people. I don't know about you, but when I was in school, I got stressed out about tests. When someone has a test in martial arts, they quite often will get stressed over that, but the words evaluation and assessment don't seem to hold nearly as much impact in that way. You could not change anything else about it, but when someone doesn't pass an evaluation, that is not nearly as harsh as saying someone failed a test, and that can give instructors a little more leeway to evaluate students more frequently and to be okay with not passing them on to the next rank, and it can give the students a little more freedom to accept and understand that, "okay, I'm not ready."

My last thought on this general overview of rank is the idea of the black belt. In some martial arts, it is a gold belt or sash, and it might not even be black. It is generally the case, however, that in nearly every martial art there is some colored indicator, something that showcases the progression from the junior ranks to the senior ranks. If not, there is likely some delineation of solid proficiency in the system, and we are going to refer to that as a black belt because it is the term that most people would accept, and everyone knows what it means. When we look at rank and testing, we need to keep that black belt special, because the rest of the world, including non-martial artists, holds some mystique in the way that they look at that rank. If we allow that to fade, we lose the most visible symbol of the martial arts. That symbol is so prominent that it is adopted as progress levels outside of martial arts. There are black belts in certain marketing and business skills. They've borrowed that from the martial arts because everyone knows what a black belt means, so we need to guard that, we need to protect that because it is incredibly valuable.

Paradox of Rank

When we get right down to it, rank within the martial arts is a paradox. Not just the belt itself, or the patch, or the sash, or whatever you use in your martial arts style to express rank, but the overall concept of rank is a contradiction. In the next section we will talk about the history of rank and where that started with Jigorō Kanō in Judo, but for now, know that in the grand scheme of martial arts, rank is a relatively new concept. It's barely 100 years old.

As much as we treasure rank, it sometimes leads to arguments. People lose friends; they split off from martial arts schools and start their own. At the end of the day, however, we are the same person whether we are wearing that belt or not. It doesn't matter how many stripes are on my belt. If I take off that belt, I'm the same person. I think that's the point. The belt, the sash, the patch, it's a symbol. We take care of it. We hold value in it. It's an outward expression of our skill, our dedication, and commitment to not only the martial arts but our personal development through martial arts. Why do we put so much respect, so much credibility into that external symbol? In most cases, it is simply because that's what we have been taught to do.

There are martial arts schools popping up that don't use belts. They don't use rank. They simply train in the way that you might in a fitness class. That doesn't mean that the personal development aspects are lost, but I don't think they are as easy to achieve. With belts, despite the problems that they cause, they give us stages of progress, they help us understand what is next, and they allow us to focus on certain things that are required for that progression, and that is an important aspect of development. We also see it in academics, a place where development and growth are so paramount.

The physical belt has some paradoxes as well. We wrap it around our waist, we sweat on it, we bleed on it. I've been a part of some schools where you are prohibited from washing it. You are prohibited from letting it touch the floor if you're not wearing it. Aren't those contradictory? If I value something, if something is important, and a representative physical symbol that I need to treat with an almost religious quality, why wouldn't I want to take care of it? I'm not saying whether you should wash your belt. That's between you and your instructor and dependent on how you do things in your school and your style, but there are times that I look at my belt, and I contemplate what it means.

At the end of the day, that belt is the external symbol of your training. It is the thing that doesn't change. You might wear different uniforms, and you will take it off, but it still represents all the time and effort that you have put into progress in your art. The blood, the sweat, the stains, the fraying, that's all indicative of the effort, time, growth, and that external symbol can, and I would say should, be valued.

As I've gotten older, as I've grown as a martial artist, that symbol becomes more important to me. On the one hand, it is something that wraps around my waist - it figuratively in the martial arts holds up my pants - but if my house was on fire, it's the first physical possession that I would grab to save. It's the one thing that I really can't replace. Yes, I have memories, and some of those memories are represented by photographs, and pieces of paper, and yearbooks, and such, but I didn't invest decades of my life into the creation of those photos or yearbooks. That belt, as it is, is the result of my training, and I can't replicate that.

We value the belt because it's a symbol of our effort in a way that very few things in the world could duplicate. Martial arts as something that gives back what you put in allows us to invest that time, that growth, and the belt shows us what we've done. However, it can get dogmatic when you value the belt too much when you would do anything to add another stripe or when you start trading or buying rank from others - yes, unfortunately it does happen - because it *is* just a piece of cloth.

History of Rank

There was a time where people were doing martial arts without belts. Martial arts rank as we know it presently really isn't that old. We can go back to Jigorō Kanō and the year of 1883. If you don't know the name, Kanō is the father of Judo. He adapted Judo from Jiu-Jitsu and turned it into its own style. Prior to the ranking system that he devised; rank was certificates as you might see in academics. He devised the system of belts.

Once introduced, there were only two colors - white and black. The original intention of the black belt back then was to show competency, not mastery, but competency in the style's basic techniques and principles. That's really all it is - it's an external symbol. In time, other martial arts styles adopted the belt system, they started to change it, add colors, add stripes, and that's great. This is the progress that leads to the belt systems we see today.

It was in 1935 that another judoka, Mikinosuke Kawaishi, stared assigning colored belts at his school. He felt that the western students that he was teaching in Paris would have more success with an external symbol of their achievement. Later, it was Gichin Funakoshi who adopted the Judo gi (the uniform) and the belts and colored rank system as he developed his style of Karate.

There's a militaristic element in the way that we handle belts. If you look at a military uniform, there's usually some indication of rank, be it bars, stars, something that shows this is where this person fits into this organization. In martial arts, we generally have the same thing.

In Japanese, the first-degree black belt is generally referred to as a Shodan, and that literally means "first step." *Sho* means first, *dan* means step, the first step. I've heard that correlated with the idea of a bachelor's degree coming out of a university, and I think that's a good way to think of it.

Knowing the history of rank isn't terribly important, but I think it is relevant. It's relevant because we often get so caught up in rank that I think it's important to realize that martial arts existed for quite a long time before rank, which means rank is not necessary for martial arts. It may be a core component of what we know martial arts to be today, but I think there's more harm than benefit in getting caught up in rank and what it means. The next time you put on your belt or your sash or whatever is that external symbol of your progress in your martial arts development, see it, honor it, give it the respect it deserves, but realize that you are exactly the same person and just as valuable when you take it off.

Benefits, Privileges and Responsibilities

Martial arts rank has so many nuances. There's the paradox of it, there's the benefit of it, and with rank comes both privilege and responsibility. Having a title, having a certain standing in a martial arts school, or really anywhere in the world doesn't give us the right to do whatever we want. It certainly confers some rights, but generally, the bigger those rights, the greater the flexibility, the more responsibility it should and usually does carry with it. Martial arts are no exception.

Martial artists are people, and people are flawed. You don't have to look too far to find an example of a martial artist who despite skill and rank and lots of time training has still failed in some way, whether they failed in their personal life, their martial arts life, or their professional life. We're all people, and because martial arts are a personal development way of life, it can be easy to forget that the people who reach the highest levels aren't necessarily the best. We don't know where they started. That growth can sometimes come from a very, very low place to start, and reaching up doesn't necessarily mean that you reach the top.

There are standards to achieve any rank. Depending on the school and the rank, it may have something to do with skill, time training, certain achievements whether those are competitive or otherwise, but in most schools any sort of eye towards personal growth is incredibly subjective, and sometimes just assumed, and that can lead to people progressing through rank without becoming good people.

I feel strongly that most martial artists, the vast majority, become better people. Unfortunately, not everyone does. There are exceptions. In those cases, it can be really conflicting to figure out how to handle this person, this exemplary martial artist who maybe has a great deal of skill and rank, but personally one might find them repulsive.

There are martial artists I know and respect in a lot of ways, but I would never have them at my dinner table. There are people who are wonderful in technique, maybe they are even great instructors, but I find some of their personal decisions to be reprehensible. How does one handle that? The way I found to reconcile those two conflicting perspectives is to compartmentalize my respect. I can respect someone's technique without respecting who they are as a person. I can respect their rank and show honor to them, but I don't have to honor who they are as a human being. Trust me, that's challenging, but it can be done, and it's something that I have to practice. As whistlekick grows, as I travel, as I meet a lot of people, as a lot of people want to talk to me, I'm occasionally now confronted with people who, for professional reasons, I need to talk to. Without whistlekick, I would block them, figuratively or maybe even literally.

Some people say that they demand respect. I don't think you can do that. Respect can only be given. I can act in a way that seems to show respect. I can bow to people, I can speak kindly to them, I can honor their achievements, but it doesn't necessarily mean that I want to. I do it out of obligation. Respect isn't something that is obligated. Respect is something that is gifted.

Along with both privileges and responsibilities, rank carries rights, particularly for instructors. Instructors have the right to teach their class in the way that they want to, the way that they feel is best. They have the right to use their judgment to foster the growth of their students and their martial arts school. They have the right to be compensated for sharing their knowledge. They don't have to be compensated, and plenty of martial arts instructors take little to no money, but they have the right if they choose. They have the right to continue their own development outside of instructing. Just because someone is a martial arts instructor doesn't mean that is all they do, or not necessarily all they should do or must do. They have the right to be treated respectfully by their students. Again, that doesn't mean that respect is genuine, but it should be conferred in at least some kind of hollow way because that's part of the structure of what we do. (As an aside, if you're a student and you don't respect your instructor, you probably need a new school.)

What *don't* instructors have the right to do? They don't have the right to act without integrity. Integrity is a broad brush, but I think we all know what it means. Also, instructors don't have the right to shirk their responsibilities. The core responsibility of a martial arts instructor is to foster the growth of their students. Anything that does not foster that growth is outside of that responsibility. When an instructor takes on a student, that student's development, at least within the timeframe of class, that student's instruction and growth is the most important thing.

What responsibility does a martial arts instructor have? Separate from the rights, an instructor's responsibility is to continue their own personal growth, the growth of their martial art, and to foster the growth of those around them. To say it even simpler, a martial arts instructor should be a beacon for martial arts and personal growth. This is especially true for lower ranks. This is part of why an instructor will generally spend more time with their lower-ranked students; they need the most help. The further along the path we get as martial artists, the more responsibility we can take for our own personal growth, just like a child. Parents have to spend the most time with the youngest children generally because they are least able to take care of themselves.

Any action of a martial arts instructor should fall within the rights and responsibilities that I've mentioned. Anything outside of that is probably extraneous, maybe even damaging. Let me give you some examples.

- Charging $500 a month for martial arts classes sounds crazy, but if people are willing to pay that, there is nothing wrong with that. It's a contract between the instructor and the student. If everyone is happy, there's nothing wrong with that. Charging $5000 for a black belt club membership that doesn't give any additional training or benefit violates the idea of integrity. It does not foster the growth of the students.

- How about mandating the frequency with which a student trains? Absolutely. Instructors have the right to make certain requirements of the students in their school. If the students don't want to play by those rules, they don't have to be there. Perfectly acceptable.

- Requiring a certain amount of homework or activities to be done outside of class? This is a weird one, but again, totally fine, because instructors have the right to set parameters for their students.

- Here's a controversial one. Preventing someone from training at another school or attending a seminar? Maybe. It depends on the instructor's reason. If the instructor doesn't want someone training at another school because it might make that instructor look bad, that's not okay. That's not integrity. If the instructor is making that judgment because the student spends too much time bouncing around and is not learning the things that they claim to want to learn, and the instructor is trying to help them focus, that is totally acceptable.

It can be easy for a martial arts instructor to go power-hungry. When you have a group of people around you who love you, look up to you, want to hear what you say and think, have you teach them, and they are willing to give you money for that, that can be pretty awesome, and it can be overwhelming. If you're not ready for that, it can get the best of you. I've seen it happen. I know what it was like when I was a martial arts instructor and had my own school. I was young. I was 22, 23 at the time, and I had some challenges with it. I don't think I violated anything, but there were temptations, and I'm glad that I didn't succumb to them.

Unfortunately, bigger temptations and different constitutions of character may allow people to violate their integrity, to not maintain the rights and responsibilities. Ideally, if martial arts students are aware of these rights and responsibilities, and they act accordingly, the bad instructors, hopefully, will stop teaching because they will lose all their students. I see martial arts as a free market economy. As people understand what they want and what they need out of martial arts, and they find the instructors that deliver that in the way they want it, the best will rise, and the others will fall away.

You can't hide poor martial arts behind rank or title

Part 8 – Etiquette and Integrity

Overview

Within the martial arts, etiquette, politeness, or whatever you want to call it is fundamental. We bow, we have a significant number of things that we do to show respect to ourselves, to our instructor, to our training partners, sometimes to the physical space that we are in, our uniform, belt, weapons, things that we do in competition. If you were to make a list of all the things that are generally part of the code of conduct within martial arts schools, it's a pretty long list. It's probably a longer list than you will see in almost any other pursuit.

We cannot operate a martial arts school without some level of formality - rank, uniform, title. I don't think any single one of them is critical or necessary, but something has to be there to have personal development. That is what martial arts are. You have to have some parameters, otherwise it just becomes freeform. You have to have some structure to progress because without it you don't know where you are or where you are going. These external symbols like rank, they can help make that process simpler. Everyone understands their role better.

That code of conduct is necessary. It is fundamental to the martial arts, to our upbringing, to our understanding of our place within the martial arts and within our martial arts school. There's a reason we have a hierarchy - hierarchy of rank, of forms, of knowledge - and that hierarchy stays in place because we respect it, and that is part of etiquette.

What is etiquette? Etiquette is a set of rules that help everyone know how to act. That etiquette, that cultural norm of the martial arts, can vary depending on the style you train, where you train, the instructor, and their lineage. It varies depending

124

on the country you are in because some cultural norms come from the country where you train.

If we boil it all down and really dig into etiquette, what is it based on? It's based on respect. When I bow to someone, I'm showing them respect, whether it is for what they are about to teach me, or that we are about to work together, hopefully, so that they can teach me something. When we shake someone's hand on the street, that's really showing respect. If I hug someone, maybe that's out of love, but part of love is respect.

Respect is so important because of the nature of what we do. Most martial arts schools are engaged in practices that have some risk, and you must trust the people around you, both your instructor and your fellow training partners. It's easier to trust someone when you respect them. If you respect someone and they mess up, it's easier to let that go. I don't know if you have ever trained with someone you don't like or respect, but it's hard to trust those people.

Those rules of etiquette can vary wildly. For example, in the Karate school that I grew up in, it was not acceptable for your belt to touch the floor unless you were wearing it. This was a significant rule. It was something we talked about. That belt was a symbol of our time. We didn't wash it; we didn't do anything to alter it. Then, I started training in Tae Kwon Do in a school where that rule doesn't exist. It was weird for me at first, but the rules of etiquette were different. If a Tae Kwon Do person showed up at that Karate school I trained in and they put their belt on the floor, they weren't doing it to be disrespectful. It was simply a different etiquette than what they knew.

Even now, when I train in other martial arts, I don't let my belt touch the floor unless I am wearing it. I haven't let go of that. In holding to that rule when I train elsewhere, I'm not doing it to be disrespectful. I'm not saying that the rules in that school that permit putting the belt on the floor are wrong. I'm saying that because what I'm doing isn't harming anyone else, it's okay. I have a slightly different code of etiquette for myself, but if I was to teach in that school, I would not teach that rule. I would not say others must adhere to that rule as I would if I was teaching based on my original Karate curriculum.

If you are visiting, if you are traveling, or if you are unsure of etiquette, the easiest thing to do is watch and mimic what other people are doing. Ask questions, and when in doubt, bow. Bowing is always a sign of respect. I have never been to a martial arts school that didn't have bowing. I have never been to a martial arts school where if you show the intent for respect that anyone would get mad at you. If I bow and then I completely screw up by asking an inappropriate question, it's probably going to be okay. Someone will correct me, and I will never do it again, but they will know that my intention was good.

Remain humble. The best example of this is always to introduce yourself by name. I don't think it's appropriate for people to introduce themselves by their rank. That rank, that title, should be asked. When people ask me my name, if I'm teaching, my response depends on the context. If someone says, "What is your name?" I will tell them my name is Jeremy. Sometimes I'll tell them my full name, and if appropriate, I will tell them, "But while we are training here, you should call me (this)," because I am honoring the code of etiquette that the instructor has set down, because I respect that instructor and their rules enough that I am not going to change them. I trust them and their process in teaching their students, and I am going to hold to their rules even if they are a little bit different from my own.

Finally, you must figure out what your own code of etiquette is. We all have a personal code, the things that are important to us, the way we live our lives, and to bring that code into your martial arts training is not only okay, but I would also say it is important. It helps you understand what martial arts mean to you and what your life means outside of your training because of martial arts. If part of your code doesn't jive with the school you are training in, you either need to find a way to reconcile those two, or it's time to find another school, or maybe it's time to look at your own personal code and contemplate a shift.

When in Rome

We've all heard the saying, "When in Rome, do as the Romans do," and when you dig right into it, it's about respect. When you train at someone else's martial arts school, or you start over in a new style or system, you want to make sure that you are doing as they do, because there is a strong possibility that you will learn something. Even if what you are doing is counter to what you are used to, recognize that there is no one right way, and if you truly want to get the most out of being somewhere else, you have to do things the way they are doing them. Be open-minded. Assume, even recognize, that you don't know everything.

The best thing you can do for your own education and the beneficial spread of martial arts is to show up for class every single time, whether it's your own school or another school, with a willingness to learn. Don't assert your own ego. Don't go in looking to prove that what you do and how you do it is better. Even if you have decades of experience, even if you are a very high-ranking martial artist, you don't have the right to enforce your own "rules" into a school that is not your own.

There is incredible wisdom in a willingness to learn from people that you don't know, from people that aren't in your own system, your own style, whether you look at it as cross-training or simply visiting others in fellowship. This is one of the things that we need more of in the martial arts. Be an ambassador, not only for your system, your style, but for yourself, your family, and for the martial arts overall.

If you don't understand the way things are done or why they are done, or if you think you have a better way, assume that there may be something you could learn, and respectfully approach the instructors, probably after class, and ask them why. Assume that you are wrong in the way you present yourself, and you will come across with humility. "I might be wrong, but why are you doing this differently than the way I do this? Please, educate me."

Remember that all martial arts started from a place of comparison, from assembling ideas from other martial arts. Offer yourself and the place that you are visiting or training at the opportunity to learn. We are all best when we learn from each other.

Respecting Elders

Respect is paramount in the martial arts. I don't think there is anyone that argues that. When we look up to someone, whether it is by age, or rank, or experience, or a combination of those, we are respecting them. We are honoring their legacy. One of my favorite definitions of the word sensei, the term in Japanese that is generally translated as teacher, is, "one who has come before." I like that.

Martial arts are so nuanced that often times we are respecting people because they have more experience, just because they have seen and done things that we haven't, or they have done those things for a longer period of time. In other industries, people are respected for their achievements, often *only* for their achievements, but in martial arts, there are plenty of people who are well-respected because they have simply put in the time. They have showcased their passion for their training, for others, for the martial arts in general, and that is something that tends to resonate for most of us.

Some people say that in martial arts we demand or expect respect, but the funny thing about respect is that you can't demand it. You can't force it in any way. You can force respectful-seeking actions, but you can't impact the spirit in which they are done. Just because someone is older, or has a higher rank, or has done things, they don't automatically deserve respect, and inherently we know that. Unfortunately, even when deserved, not everyone gives respect. It's free will.

We all know the difference between genuine and fake respect. We have seen it. We have experienced it. Maybe we have even given it ourselves. Quite often when we use the term respect, we use it as a blanket term, "I respect that person," but respecting someone doesn't mean that you respect everything about them, and I think that this is the key for most of us to remember. I respect Chuck Norris for his amazing martial arts accomplishments. I don't respect him as a surgeon. I would love to take a seminar with him, but I'm not going to ask him to remove my appendix. Does that mean I'm not respectful of him? Of course not, but I respect certain elements.

There are martial artists that deserve respect for their accomplishments, or their ability to teach, or their rank only. Unfortunately, just as with people who are non-martial artists, martial artists are fallible. We can respect elements of what people say or think or do without respecting the entire person. There are martial artists I respect only in certain ways. I think they are terrible people. Compartmentalizing is an important part of making sure that you are treating the appropriate people with the appropriate respect at the appropriate times. Let's be honest, there are times when you must fake respect. It's easier than getting in an argument. It's easier than having a misunderstanding or even being ostracized from a group. If you don't respect your instructor, however, you should probably find a new school.

Of the different kinds of respect, of all the ways you can show respect, self-respect is the most important. If you find you don't respect yourself, it's probably the thing you need to work on the most, even beyond any physical skills or other elements of your training. Self-respect is ultimately who you are. No one will ever treat you better than you treat yourself.

Respect can never be demanded. You can enforce action, but you can never mandate the spirit behind the action. If you want someone's respect, earn it.

Part 9 – Teaching

Everyone Has Something to Teach

Everyone has something to teach. That is a statement I first heard from my original Karate instructors when I was a kid, and I didn't fully understand it at the time. The idea that everyone could teach me something about martial arts struck me as completely ridiculous when I first heard it. I dismissed it. "What about someone on the first day of their training? What are they going to teach me? That's crazy." Then, years later, as I taught and trained with people on their very first day of martial arts, I learned. I learned A LOT. I learned that no matter what you say, no matter what you do, no matter how you show someone a movement, they will find a way to do it weird and different, and maybe even hit you with it. That blew my mind. Everyone DOES have something to teach, even if what they are teaching you is that you have room to improve in your instruction, or that a certain technique can be done in a way that you never even imagined.

Martial arts are about growth, continuous growth, and no one can attain perfection. The moment you think you're perfect, you are wrong, and you stop learning. You must be open to learning. You must accept your own failing. No one can always execute a technique perfectly, and even if you have done something for that 10,000 hours that gets kicked around, maybe you can be considered an expert, but it doesn't mean you're done learning. If we do that math on that 10,000 hours, that master level, for most of us it will take at least 20 years. In fact, with a lot of people's training schedule, it's 40 to 50 years, which is why I struggle with that term *master* as it is used in martial arts.

When you are training, try to maintain the white belt mentality, the idea that there is nearly an infinite amount for you to learn, that what you have learned already, what you know, is a drop in the bucket. Empty your cup, to use that cliché. Consider every single point of view. Remember, every point of view comes from something. It may come from a misunderstanding, but where did that misunderstanding come from? If someone gets three or four years into their training, and they are doing a movement wrong, how did they learn it wrong? Someone taught them wrong, or someone allowed them to continue practicing wrong. If you are the instructor, maybe you didn't teach it to them directly, but someone you taught did.

When we let that go and recognize that we are all trying to learn, it means that we are all trying to teach. We are teaching ourselves, and we are teaching those around us. If I am lined up in class, and someone to the side of me is observing what I'm doing, I'm teaching them, not directly, but the way I do something matters. They assume I'm doing it right, and they're trying to better themselves based on my movements. Maybe they spaced out for a moment and didn't hear what the instructor was saying. I have to make sure that I'm paying attention, for them and for me.

One of the great things about martial arts is that we are all trying to help each other learn. It doesn't matter if you are a white belt on your first day, because even in that role, you are helping the instructor better their skills at teaching. We all have something to teach. Consider the ridiculous example of someone who is a complete moron, someone who can't connect the dots to save their life, and they ask completely foolish questions that maybe don't even relate to martial arts. Let's imagine something that extreme. You can learn compassion. They can teach you to be more compassionate for them and their ignorance, or their foolishness. You can learn patience. That is still learning. That is still them teaching you.

Growing as a martial artist doesn't just mean that you are developing skills. It means that you are becoming more compassionate and empathetic. You are getting better at teaching, and you are getting better at learning. Learning is a skill. Look at the way other people teach. Look at the way other people learn. You can observe both and improve your skills. Some people learn certain things better than others, but that doesn't mean that there aren't things you can learn better than other people. The more you understand the way you learn, and the way other people learn, the better you can teach to different people. The better you are teaching different kinds of people, the better you will be at learning from different kinds of instructors. Yes, it's a circle.

Your way isn't the only way. Maybe it's the best way for that situation, but it may not be the best way overall. There are other ways to consider, and if you are open-minded, you can improve. The moment you close that mind off, you are done. You have capped out as to how much knowledge you are going to gain. If you think you know it all, you are literally done learning.

Starting a School

Starting a martial arts school is something a lot of martial arts students will consider even long before it is time. When you start martial arts and are maybe a blue belt, a yellow belt, maybe even a white belt or a brand new student, and you're engaged in this practice that changes your life, it's only natural that you may consider sharing that passion with others down the line. Not everyone that starts martial arts as a white belt is going to make it far enough that they are going to achieve the skill and rank to open their own school, but if you do, it can be a very big, sometimes overwhelming decision, and not every martial arts school opens for the same reasons.

I used to have a martial arts school. I taught Karate for a couple of years right after college. I did it as something to further my own training, put a little bit of money in my pocket, and give back, pretty much the same reasons right about the same time of life that my Karate instructors started teaching me. After a couple of years, I started building an IT company, my first business, and I didn't have time to run this martial arts school. More importantly, I didn't have the energy. I would show up to class at the end of the day, ready to teach, but I was exhausted. I saw the impact that was having on me, on my ability to teach at the level I felt was necessary, and most importantly, on my students. They weren't getting my best, so I decided to shut it down.

There are lots of reasons you shouldn't teach martial arts, and there are lots of things you shouldn't do while teaching martial arts. Let's go over some of those first. If you reduce the standards, the quality of your instruction, simply to make money or make more money, you should not be doing that. If you believe you are not qualified to teach, you shouldn't be teaching. That is not the same thing as saying you aren't good at teaching, because there are plenty of people who are great teachers, but because they are constantly critical of themselves, they don't see the skills that they bring to their students.

One of the most polarizing subjects in the world of martial arts, and THE most polarizing subject when you start talking about teaching is whether martial arts should be taught for money. Should there be a financial exchange? Personally, I believe so, but there are a lot of other people who don't think so. We've covered this on our podcast. We've had guests on, we've talked about the way they handle teaching for money or not for money. I'm not going to say there is a right or wrong answer here. I have my opinion, but it's based on my own experiences and my own goals. Even as I write this book, one of my goals is to expand and grow the martial arts, and it's hard to grow something if money isn't involved.

Teaching martial arts could be a full-time job, or it could be a part-time job. There is no right or wrong here either. I don't have data to back it up, but I suspect most martial arts schools, at least in the United States, are part-time. By maintaining a full-time job elsewhere, you have diversified income, you have something to fall back on if the school goes through a rough patch, and you probably have other benefits that are helpful. To me the most important benefit is that teaching martial arts can remain something you do simply because you love it. It never becomes something you have to do in that way you have to go to work. If work is martial arts, you must go to that school and you must teach.

On the flipside, when you are a full-time martial arts school, you can offer so much more to your students. There are so many things you can give them. You can have classes in the morning or the middle of the day. You can focus on being the best instructor possible, and on building the best school possible. You can grow as a martial artist, as a business owner, and as an instructor, right alongside your students.

Here are five reasons I think every long-term martial artist should at least consider starting their own school and teaching.

1. To give back and to spread the martial arts.
2. To further develop your skills. If you've spent much time teaching, you know what I'm talking about. You get good at teaching some very fundamental things quickly. You have to because people learn in such different ways.
3. You improve the lives of others. I would say this can be addictive. I've watched martial arts instructors and the joy they take in watching people grow, not just as martial artists but as human beings. To know you have a part in that is so powerful.

4. To give you a career you can feel good about. Whether or not it's a full-time job, you can still feel good about the time you are investing.
5. The final reason: to make money. What's better than doing something you love and making money with it?

Now that we've gone over some of the reasons why to have a martial arts school, let's talk about how to start one. There are franchises available, and starting a franchise is straight-forward. You go through some training, you understand the business practices, and then you open. You have to pay some money and there are ongoing fees, but from that you get ongoing support. I don't know anything about the ins and outs of any of the martial arts franchises available, so I'm not going to recommend them. I'm also not going to suggest that they are a bad idea because if I don't understand something, I can't tell you anything about it, good or bad.

I can say that many people who are going to open a martial arts school are going to do so without any kind of franchise. Whether or not they realize it, it's because they have ideas they want to try out and implement. There are things they want to do differently from their instructors. While this can cause tension in the martial arts world, this is also a natural part of the development of every one of us as martial arts students.

Here are six different models you can use to open your martial arts school.

1. It can be part-time in some type of shared space, maybe a community center, church basement, multi-function room, dance hall, something like that. This is the easiest way to start. It's the lowest expense. You don't have to worry about taxes on the building. You don't have to worry about too much. You have your time slot, you advertise it, you show up, you teach, collect money, repeat. You can focus on growing the program, and you get to keep your day job. However, you don't have full control of the space. You won't be able to design it how you want. You won't be able to put up heavy bags and leave them there. If you want to use mats as part of your martial arts program, you'll probably have to put them away at the end of the day. That can be inconvenient, but this is a great way to start, and this is the way that I think, from my observations, most martial arts instructors start.

2. While less common, there is also a full-time shared space. This would be something where you are renting the space, but maybe there are things that happen during the off times. Maybe your program runs from noon through 8 pm. You have lunchtime classes, maybe fitness kickboxing, and then you've got kids classes starting in the afternoon, then your evening classes, but maybe during the mornings there are other programs that run there. This doesn't happen too often. Usually, when a school

gets to the point where they have that many hours of classes, they look at having their own private space, something they don't have to share. There is a lot of benefit in not having to worry about the upkeep of a building, and of course, if you share a space, it's going to be less expensive than if you have exclusive use of it. The biggest downside I see to sharing a space is that it's not as professional. There is a perception. If people see that you share your space with a dance school and half a dozen other things, they are not going to believe you are successful as a martial arts instructor. It's not necessarily bad, but at some point, you will probably lose prospective students, especially if you are near full-time schools. Being aware of this and being smart with the numbers and trying to grow into a full-time space of your own is going to be the goal for some martial arts instructors.

3. The next option is being a full-time instructor and owning your space. Whatever that building is, you own it, your name is on it, sometimes you own it and lease it back to your martial arts school as separate businesses. There are a lot of different financial arrangements you can do. You probably want to talk to an accountant or maybe even an attorney on how to handle this stuff. That's far beyond the scope of this book, but it can be very profitable to do this. All that money that you would spend giving it to someone else every month, you don't have to give it to anyone else anymore. There

is a lot more responsibility, but this is the goal for a lot of martial arts instructors, to grow their program so large, so profitably, that they get to have their own space.

4. Numerous schools don't worry about the ownership part of the building. They lease that space, but they are still full-time. This can be a very good option because the initial cash outlay to buy a building is huge, especially something large enough for a good full-time martial arts school. Leasing takes a commitment. It's often three or five years. I've even seen some ten-year leases, but you don't have to worry about any of the upkeep. That can be good and bad. If you have a good landlord, things work out well. If you don't... ugh... you could be in trouble.

5. Uncommon, but I have seen it, and it can be great, is running a program as an employee by finding an organization that wants to offer martial arts. This could be some mixed-use gym, fitness center, boys and girls club, things like that. I've seen this happen where you go in, and you say, "Hey, I want to start a martial arts program," and you get all of their marketing power, they pay you a salary, but you are not the boss. This is one of the big challenges with this format, is that you have people looking over your shoulder, telling you whether they are happy with the way you are doing things. The financial arrangement you have, your salary, may or may not be impacted by the number of students you have,

but if you are the type of person who likes to get up, go to work, get things done, and not have to worry about as much when you leave, this could be a good option.

6. The last option is buying an existing school. This typically happens if you've been training in that school or at least in that system. I've seen people slowly buy in - buy 5% here, another 10% later, and so on. They are becoming more invested in that school, and then finally, as the school owner maybe gets older, wants to retire, move, maybe do something else, they will sell the remainder to that person, or sometimes to a group of people. The upside here is you know exactly what you get. The downside, it can be harder to make your own way. It's also one of the more expensive options.

At the beginning of this section, I talked about things that you shouldn't do as an instructor when you are considering teaching and owning a martial arts school, but let's end with the things that you should. You should enjoy it. You should create an environment in which your students are drawn. You should focus on delivering the best quality instruction you can and not the money because when you focus on giving people a great education, a wonderful space, and the best instruction from passionate instructors, they'll want to come. They'll want to keep coming, and they'll bring their friends, and the money follows. If you focus on the money, the other stuff doesn't necessarily show up. It's an ironic positioning in the world. The more we focus on money, the less we seem to have it. The more we focus on things that lead to money, the happier we are and the more money we seem to have. This holds true in martial arts and in teaching martial arts, so keep that in mind.

Summer Camps and Different Environments

Martial arts can happen anywhere. It does not have to happen within the four walls of your typical training hall. That doesn't just mean that martial arts are some mental and emotional pursuit and that it happens at home... No. I'm not talking about that. I'm talking about training, actual, physical training, outside of where you normally train. This tends to fall into two categories - summer camps and different training environments.

Let's start talking about summer camps, which we can also think about as destination training, the idea that you go somewhere, and you stay there for a little while, a couple of days, maybe a week, maybe more, and you train. The focus of your time is training. The other things that happen must happen, like sleeping and eating. Maybe there is even a social component. These aren't just for children. I've seen weekend-long, even multi-week programs for adults. Quite often, they involve traveling to the country of origin for the martial art. Maybe you're going to Thailand to train Muay Thai, Okinawa to train Karate, or China to train Kung Fu. These can be expensive, but they can also be very fun and beneficial.

When you are training in a different place, you are going to see things differently. You can have different training partners and different instructors. Your mind is open because things are so new that you are avoiding this routine mentality. If you have been training for more than a couple of years, you've probably realized that you train with a lot of the same people, in the same space, with the same instructors, even facing the same way. While that isn't necessarily boring, it doesn't light up this novel aspect that our brain craves. When that's on, it tends to be easier to learn.

Variety is incredibly valuable to your training, not just specific techniques or specific forms, but overall. It builds excitement, keeps your mind engaged. At these events, you get to meet new people, and, as you may know, developing friendships creates more opportunities, more connections, which is good for you, and it's good for the martial arts. These connections break down barriers. We see things pop up out of friendship and connection. This could be businesses, it could be more training opportunities, and sometimes it's relationships. There are people get married because they meet at training seminars. I know some of them.

I'm a big fan of destination training. Whether you call it a summer camp or vacation, it is a great opportunity to help you dive more in-depth with your art. When you go to a destination, you get to forget about other things that would normally be a distraction from such detailed focus. For many of us, to leave our day job, go to our training a few days a week, it takes some time to transition out of the stress of the day. If that takes you 20 minutes of training, and you have an hour-long class, well, you've just lost a third of the high-quality training you could have had.

Contrast that with the opportunity to train for a weekend. Let's say training is 10 hours a day, or even 4 hours a day. You get a month's worth of training in just a couple days by transitioning in and remaining in that space, that environment with all those other people that are there for the same reason, and you get a lot more very high-quality training. By having more time outside of the regular class schedule, you can go super deep on more aspects of your art, such as forms. You can spend 2 hours working on a form, and the instructors aren't going to feel like they are "wasting" your time. How often does it feel appropriate to work on a single form this way in a general weekday class? It would be the entire class. If you don't like that form, or if you don't know that form, you're in trouble. However, if a class spends a couple of hours on that form during a camp, you have time for everybody to learn that form, to work on it, to understand the application, and so much more.

Let's talk about training in different environments, what we are going to call field trips. Your surroundings have a tremendous amount to do with the energy that you invest in your training. As I said in the last section, if you are in the same place every time, you might find that your engagement falls off a bit. Simply taking the class outside, to a different school, the backyard, or a parking lot can have a huge impact on people's engagement. They'll act differently. They'll see things differently. They'll do things differently. When I teach children's classes, I will often have them turn 90 degrees every 15 minutes or so. It's the same space, but by facing a different wall, they have a different response. It can be that simple. You can even use different lighting. Little things like that which seem trivial can have a huge impact. The more time you've spent in that space, the more important changing things up can be, and the bigger results you will see.

It is important to mix it up because it keeps people learning, and it shows them what it is like to use martial arts, even just in training, when they're uncomfortable or otherwise outside of their comfort zone. Here is a list of places that you can train outside of the ordinary. Not all of these are appropriate for a class, but they are all good to consider for training: you can train in a car; public park; go into the woods; at a beach; in a pool; in front of your house, yes, especially if people can see you; in a bedroom; on top of something tall, which could be a mountain, or it could be standing on a pole, like in The Karate Kid. Any of those places could be used during the day or at night, while it's hot, while it's cold, in the dark, in bright lights, outside during a rainstorm, in the snow, etc. If you operate a school that has air conditioning, you know how different it can be if that air conditioning gives out. Every one of those is going to have different results, and those different results come from the opportunities not only in what you can do but how you are going to feel in that situation.

I'm not suggesting you do anything unhealthy, anything that is going to put your physical body at risk, but to train while you are uncomfortable is a great benefit for you. While training on your front lawn, others might see you. With cars going by and looking at the "weirdo" doing martial arts in the front yard, most of us are going to feel uncomfortable. Working through that is a big deal because if you can work through that on your own, you are more likely to pull out your martial arts in a crowded situation if you need it.

Information Overload

How much stuff should we know? How much should we be teaching? These are important questions, and there is no right answer. Considering the question and understanding the implications has a huge impact on you and your martial arts, and if you're teaching, on the martial arts of those you're teaching.

Some instructors, especially new instructors, seem to want to teach everything to their students all at once. This creates what I call information overload. We all have a certain capacity for learning, and that learning must happen at a certain speed. You can teach me one technique. You can probably teach me two or three techniques. If you try to teach me 30 techniques, I'm not going to remember all of them. I'm not going to be able to do all of them well, even if you show me a list. There is only so much that I can comprehend and internalize at one time.

One of the challenges of being an instructor is that everyone's capacity to learn is different. People learn differently, different amounts, different methods, and if we are going to keep everyone progressing, we must find ways to adapt to these differences. The more you throw at people, the less opportunity they have to learn by making mistakes. This is something that a lot of people forget when they start teaching. People learn by making mistakes. How does a child learn how to walk? By falling down. How does someone learn how to punch? By messing up that punch.

Yes, you correct, and yes, you help, but not every single repetition.

One of the easiest ways to combat information overload is by having a very fixed curriculum. I'm not necessarily a fan of this. I think every school should be run in whatever way makes sense for them, for those instructors, tor their goals, etc., but if you have a fixed curriculum, it is far easier to let people make mistakes, to avoid throwing too much new information at people, and to give them the opportunity to grow as martial artists over time. A fixed curriculum guarantees that people know what is expected of them for their next promotion, and it can make sure that the correct techniques - not too few, not too many - are taught at the right time. It also helps limit the gaps, because if you are teaching extra stuff to people, they are not learning other things. In most schools, rank promotions are a subjective thing, having a fixed curriculum can help reduce the subjectivity of those events.

The core curriculum should be small. It doesn't mean you don't build things from that, but I've looked at some of these curriculums that are like thick books. There is so much material there. It's too much. New instructors especially want to put in everything. People can't learn everything. What is the most important? If you were to start with one thing, what is the one thing you want your students to learn? That goes in. If you could only have two things you could teach them, what would those be? Start to build on those concepts. Less is more when you are educating someone. Even within a fixed curriculum, there needs to be space for people to grow individually. There must be time for people to work on their own combinations, their own understanding of the things that you are going to give them because that is a necessary component of education.

We can create a spectrum between knowledge and proficiency. The more knowledgeable someone is, the less proficient they are going to be at any one thing. If you only teach someone how to punch, and they come to martial arts class two times a week, and they spend an hour punching, they are going to be the best puncher you have ever seen. If that same person learns 12 techniques every day, they are probably going to be terrible at all of them. You have to find a balance between new information and giving people the opportunity to become proficient.

When we look at martial arts curriculum, we see that - in the good schools anyway - they don't include everything. Another way to say that is there is a style. If you look at any martial arts style, there are things that are included and not included. If you talk to those instructors of those styles, they probably know things beyond what they teach.

At any stage in training, to avoid information overload, you should be supplying only enough information to keep the students engaged and excited. By throwing out a new technique, or a new way to do it, or a new combination periodically, students stay engaged. They are happy to learn new things, but you also give them the time and space to get better at that new thing AND the old things. New things can help old things seem fresh again. If you teach someone five techniques, and you show them all the various ways that you can combine them, and then you give them a sixth, you've got a lot more combinations.

I see information overload all the time. I see it when I travel. I see it sometimes in the schools I train in. I see it at seminars. People want to share so much. They want their students to learn to be better than them, so they try to shoehorn all this knowledge into their brains, and that's not the way people learn. People learn slowly over time, which means we have to teach slowly over time, and that requires patience. That doesn't always fit with the lifestyle that we have here in the United States. The more you teach, the less they'll learn. If you watch experienced instructors, they are far more patient. They understand this. If you are a new instructor, look at the way you teach. Are you trying to teach too much? If you are a student, and you are getting bored, and you are asking for new things, have you become proficient at the stuff that you know?

Difficult Students

Teaching martial arts means you will have different types of students, and unfortunately, not every student is going to be a pleasure to teach. Yes, even in the world of martial arts, there are difficult people to deal with, and some of those people will be your students.

When we think of teaching martial arts as helping people grow - that personal development aspect and fostering it in our students - it becomes clear that those difficult students are the ones who need us the most, the ones who need the most compassion and help. Maybe something happened in their life that is making them act the way they are. There is a good chance that something is going on in their lives that makes them difficult.

It's not easy to deal with people who act out but try to have empathy for their situation. It makes things easier. One of the things that I try to do is assume that the difficult people I'm dealing with have been through one or multiple horrendous, severe actions in their lives, that there are such extenuating circumstances that the way they are acting is actually good given those circumstances. I find this level of compassion makes it much easier for me to deal with the things they do, which would otherwise make me want to pull my hair out.

When we are talking about children, we MUST be compassionate. Children have not been alive long enough to make them fully accountable for their actions. Where did they learn this behavior? They probably learned it from their parents. If you get the opportunity to work with these children, you have an amazing chance to help them outgrow what they have been taught. Children test boundaries, and difficult children REALLY test boundaries, so identifying those boundaries, making sure they are clear, and holding children to those boundaries is crucial. It's the only way they will start to trust you. Once they trust you, you can help them.

Difficult students, including children, need some one-on-one time, whether that is a couple of minutes before class to help set the expectations, maybe after class to point out where they did really well and where they can improve, maybe 30 seconds in the middle of class, or maybe you offer them a free private session once in a while. The more one-on-one time you can get with them, the better you can help them understand who they are as an individual and as a martial artist.

Childish behavior is not restricted to children. Adults act out, too. They need your compassion. They need you to communicate with them. They need to be socialized in a way that maybe they haven't been. Depending on how you run your school, it may not be appropriate for you to invite them out for coffee or a drink, but maybe you could have one of the other students do that, spend time showing them someone cares about their point of view. To understand the situation that they are experiencing can help you understand how to work with them. People want to feel cared about, and oftentimes when someone enters a new space, they will test the boundaries, just as children do. Adults will test those boundaries trying to find if people are going to care about them or is this just one more occurrence of the world rejecting them. For plenty of people, this is the reality they see, and they will try to create it around themselves, even where it doesn't exist. If you want to help them, it can be a great deal of work, but it is really rewarding. These are the people that need you the most, and if you put in even a little bit of effort, you may start to see those walls crumble. In effect, you may positively change their reality.

On the flip side, you can't let their energy occupy all your time. You have other students to work with, and you have to help them. Your responsibility is to all your students, not just one. If your efforts are helping one student, but not helping everyone else, then you have to find a different way to handle it.

I once had a young student in my children's class who didn't fit well. He needed more attention. I spoke with his parents, and we set up a time once a week for me to work with him individually. Once we had that time together, he progressed rapidly. He started to trust me, and we started to have some pretty good sessions. He learned movements, and he got better. He would test his boundaries, and I would show him where they were, show him when he was crossing those lines, and pull him back. Over time, he didn't test boundaries as much.

The sad part is you won't be able to help every student, but that doesn't mean that every student doesn't deserve your efforts to try to help them. You don't know how helpful you can be, even in a short period of time, and just because someone comes in, trains for a little while, then leaves that doesn't mean you haven't set them on a better path. It's not only the students that stay that you have benefited. For all you know, that student that comes in for a month or less of someone showing they care, that can completely change their lives. Never underestimate your impact.

Teaching Strangers

If you are an instructor, there may be times when you teach people you don't normally teach. You could be at a seminar. You could be a visiting instructor at another school, or maybe a camp. Maybe you are teaching a self-defense class in the community. Whatever the situation, teaching people you don't normally teach is dramatically different than teaching your everyday students.

I see a lot of instructors make some pretty big mistakes in this situation. They try to cram too much information into the people, or otherwise, forget that these are not their students. The best way to handle these situations to have the most impact, regardless of the goal, is to remember your "why." Why are you teaching these people? You're teaching to pass on some knowledge. You're teaching to share. Why are you NOT teaching? You are not teaching to feed your own ego, and if you are, you shouldn't be. What you are teaching doesn't need to be brand new to these people. It just needs to be your way. Own it. I could travel to any martial arts school and teach a basic punch, but I would teach it in my way. I will guarantee that almost everyone will get something different out of that, because the way I was taught a punch is different from the way they were taught a punch, and the way I've trained that punch over the years is different from the way they've trained that punch. Does it necessarily mean what I am going to teach them will be valuable and will take over for the way they've been punching? No, probably not, but exposing people to new things is fun, and if you make it fun, they are going to enjoy it. If you enjoy teaching, they will enjoy learning.

When you are teaching people that you don't get to work with frequently, the key is repetition. Start with something very, very simple. It doesn't have to be easy, but make it a single concept and drill it over and over and over again. That doesn't mean you do the same thing 500 times, but rather find 50 different ways to do the same thing ten times. Help them understand the way the technique can work in their martial arts. Use different stances, do it in place, moving forward, backward, to the sides, teach it in a sparring context, teach it in forms, teach it in whatever ways you have. By mixing it up and showing how that concept, that simple thing, can interface with everything they know and do, they are going to have the most value from your time. They are going to be thankful for you investing in them.

The opposite would be trying to throw a lot of things at people. Go back to the information overload section. That applies just as much, if not more when you are working with people who aren't your students consistently. Which would you rather have: they leave with one concept they understand well, or 30 concepts that they are going to forget tomorrow? Remember that people learn in different ways, so you want to show them, you want to tell them, you want to help them understand how it applies, you want to do things slowly, quickly, from different angles, you want them to work on it individually, with partners, in groups, you want them to teach it to each other, teach it to themselves, have time to work on it individually, and you want to ask them questions. The more different methods of education you present, the more they are going to understand it, and thus remember it, take it away, and spread that knowledge.

Don't forget what it's like to be a student. If you haven't been a student in a long time, this can be easy to forget. Being a student is scary. You don't want to mess up. You are afraid of looking foolish in front of others. Maybe even more importantly, if you are not having fun, you're probably not learning. The best education is also entertaining. If you make what you teach fun, if you enjoy teaching it, they will probably enjoy learning it. Sometimes when I'm working with people and I'm stuck, maybe the group that I have can't grasp the concept that I was asked to teach, or maybe I'm working with a group of children and they've just run out of steam, I err on the side of having fun. I would rather they leave having had a lot of fun and learning less than throw more information at them and they have less fun because if they have fun, they will come back. If they don't have fun, they might not. If they don't come back, you have NO opportunity to teach them again.

Teaching Children

In the last few sections, we've talked a lot about teaching children, and how teaching children can both be rewarding but also really challenging. Instead of revisiting that information and presenting it differently, I really want to talk about some of the unique aspects of having children in your martial arts school and the responsibilities that you may have as being part of a school that has children. It doesn't matter whether you are the owner, the chief instructor, an assistant instructor, or even a student. There are some things to being a kid these days that can be really tough. Within the martial arts, we have some unique tools, thus a responsibility to helping kids in this way.

Bullying is a whole different animal now than it was when I was a child. Bullying has always been there. It's part of human nature, but it is so much more pervasive these days. We will never exterminate bullying. We will never get to the point where people don't challenge others and push them down, literally and figuratively, but the more we understand it and the more we understand where it comes from, and the differences between natural actions that we may classify as bullying and those that are way over the line, the better we can help kids understand and grow. Unfortunately, bullying doesn't stop. It continues to happen as adults, and we want to make sure that children have the tools to handle it when they become adults and don't have others stepping in to help them.

We are human beings. We have a social structure, and part of that social structure involves testing each other to figure out the hierarchy. I'm not a big fan of hierarchy, but it happens. In any social group there are the people that everyone else looks to for leadership. These things happen, and whether we like them, they are natural, and they are part of our genetics. In fact, if we were to remove these qualities to humanity, our species would probably die off.

On the one hand, calling people names, making them feel poorly about themselves, these are things that will always exist. Calling someone a name is not assault. It probably is bullying. It depends on the context. On the other hand, you have things that are assault, and they are being labeled as bullying, and that is never okay. It has never been okay, and it is never going to be okay. Shoving a kid into a locker, that's bullying, *and* that's assault. In fact, I don't like it when we use the term bullying for things like that because I think it trivializes it.

There is no difference between me being a child in high school and putting a child into a locker, and me working a job that requires changing and me putting another employee into a locker. In the latter, it's obviously assault, but somehow in schools, it's passed off as bullying. It's something that we need to deal with, yes, but where are the consequences? Where is the legal action?

Let's imagine that you have a child that somehow you can shelter from all bullying, and then they get into the real world, and they have a boss who is incredibly demanding and uses loud and sometimes even harsh language with them. What if that boss isn't calling them names? What if that boss is just aggressive? How is that child going to react to that? They will probably fall apart. They won't be able to function in that environment. I don't know about you, but I have worked with a lot of people. I had someone just yesterday who was very upset with me, raised their voice, and threw a lot of emotions at me about something I did that they didn't like. Was it upsetting to me? Yes, but because I've dealt with that before, I was able to find a way to communicate with them and find a solution.

Bullying is part of life. We all learn through challenges. Not only is it going to happen, it has to happen. We are all facing our own battles. We can't just shed them. Part of bringing our own experiences into a social structure, into a school or the workplace, part of being a person is facing your own demons, and sometimes people work those out with other people. Kids need the opportunity to learn what it is like to become an adult. They need to challenge each other. They need to test, experiment, and learn from the results. We have to guide them. It is the job of a parent to raise an adult, to prepare a child for adulthood, not to shelter them from everything that could possibly go wrong. It is a fine line, and everyone is going to draw it differently.

As martial arts instructors, we can teach people what bullying is and is not. We have the opportunity to teach students, children, what it is like to deal with people who cross that line, understanding, "Hey, this child is trying to harm me physically. I have the right to defend myself," versus, "This other child is making me feel bad about myself. I do not have the right to harm them," and further,

"Here are some tools that I can use to reduce the impact of the actions they are taking against me."

We did an entire episode based around a news article that I once read about a school that reprimanded a child for what was genuinely an act of heroism. The school did not condone the act that this one child took, and the news article made the rounds. I was pleased to see it pop up so prominently in so many places, and it started a lot of conversations. In this news article, one child who was a martial arts student was observing a kid picking on another kid. Then he heard what he was pretty sure was the sound of a knife. He defended that third child, and yes, that other kid had a knife. He possibly saved that kid's life. We don't know what would have happened, but bottom line, there was a child who grossly crossed the line from what we could call bullying into legal, criminal action. The child defended the unarmed child and was then thrown out of school.

What bothered me so much about this news article and the occurrence it talked about was that it was conditioning people not to be heroic. This child instinctively was willing to risk harm to themselves to defend someone else. Heroism is something that we have always valued. It is something that we continue to value. We all have heroes, and the last thing that I think we should have is any kind of system that discourages heroic acts. The world would be better if there were more heroes. Why are we so drawn to superhero movies? We crave that. We want to have these people in our midst helping us.

As human beings, if we have the ability to help someone, I would say we generally have a responsibility to do it. The more severe the need, the more pressing the responsibility. As martial artists, we have the ability to help people, whether we are an adult or a child, and thus we have the responsibility. There is a fine line between being heroic and being foolish. Sometimes, they are the same thing, but in modern times we have cultivated this society that creates spectators. We videotape these actions instead of stepping in to help. We are so afraid of the consequences - and let's face it, sometimes they are trivial consequences - that we are not willing to step in. What would have happened to that child if the other kid hadn't stepped in? Would he have gotten stabbed? We don't know, but is it worth finding out? The parents of the child who was expelled, as much as they rejected the actions of the school, it is not going to change the actions of that child in the future. The parents completely supported him.

The reason people can get away with bad things is because other people around them are indifferent. Unfortunately, the policies in many schools today encourage indifference. If you observe a child taking harmful action against another child, you are not permitted to step in. You have to find an adult. It takes a long time to find an adult, and a lot can happen in that time. We can change that spectator culture. We can make sure that children understand where their responsibilities are because of their opportunities, because of the skills they learn, and when and where they use them. The more influence we have, the more opportunity we have to change that spectator culture, the more influence we have on the world, the more influence THEY have on the world.

Let's teach our children to stand up for others. Let's make valuing the lives, the health, the wellbeing of other children part of the curriculum we teach our martial arts students. The more we do that, the more people will observe the positive impact martial arts is having on the world, and the more people will train in the martial arts. If you know anything about me and anything about whistlekick, this is one of our fundamental goals. In fact, it is job number one for whistlekick, to grow and spread the martial arts.

Bullying is a growing problem because we allow it, but we don't have to. Doing good is contagious, but it takes work. We have to look for opportunities to put good back into the world, but they are there. They are constantly there. We just have to tune our eyes to see them.

Teaching Teens

Teaching teenagers is a whole different world. If you've raised a teenager, you know how challenging it can be. If you've *taught* teenagers, you REALLY know how challenging it can be. This is the age where children start to become adults, and they haven't quite figured out what that means. In other ways, especially physically, they can be adults. In a lot of older cultures, you become an adult at 13, 14, 15 years old. To have a 14- or 15-year-old in your classes means sometimes you are treating them like children, and sometimes you are treating them like adults.

In the United States, we tend to view martial arts as something children do, and there is something wrong with that marketing, because we are marketing martial arts to children, and while it isn't easy to be a kid, most of us would agree it is much harder to be an adolescent and a teenager. Martial arts have an opportunity to give this age group a reprieve from life. Teenagers struggle to fit in. They want to know where they are in the world. They crave acceptance, and it is this acceptance that means so many children that are enrolled in martial arts when they are younger drop out around age 10, 11, or 12, because they are looking to be accepted by their peers, and part of being accepted by your peers means team sports, to belong to a group.

To be a 12-year-old in a martial arts class with a bunch of 6- and 7-year-olds, you don't fit in there. To be a 12-year-old in a class with 20-, 30-, 50-year-olds, you don't fit in there either. If possible, I recommend having a teenage class. I've seen this done, and it is immensely powerful. If you can build a critical mass of teenagers, you have your own sort of team sport. You will attract teenagers from all over the place.

One of the challenges in attracting and retaining teenagers to the martial arts is that we don't have clearly defined role models. If you look at the way a lot of teenagers identify with the world and see themselves, they are on a path to doing something great, and they look up to someone else. It may be an athlete, an entrepreneur, or a scientist. In the martial arts, what role models do we have for them? We have people for them to look up to, but teenagers want to look up to someone larger than life. Unfortunately, the instructor of a school is not larger than life. They know them well.

Most teenagers, at least as they get into their later teens, have some financial responsibility. Whether that be their social life or a car, there are things that they are starting to spend money on, and they are starting to understand how money fits into their lives. How many of them see remaining in the martial arts as something that is going to be financially lucrative? Very few. Now we have taken something so powerful, something that could be so impactful during this time of their lives, and we have essentially stripped away any of the perks that would encourage them to remain in martial arts.

There are things that we can do. If we give them their own space, their own class time where it's only teenagers, they could create their own place. They can work out with their friends or people that become their friends, people to whom they can relate. These teenager classes don't have to be just for martial arts. What if there was a class that presented martial arts, but in a way that helped make them better at outside sports? What if you snuck in the lessons of martial arts under the guise of helping student-athletes become better at their chosen sport?

The way you teach a class to teenagers should be very different than the way you teach it to children and adults. Teenagers need that social dynamic in their classes, and if you don't provide it, they probably won't stick around. To have an hour-long class that involves a lot of group activities, that is where they are going to get that social component. It doesn't mean it's not a martial arts class. It doesn't mean they aren't going to learn a lot of martial arts. It does mean that they need to be able to work with each other and test each other.

Helping a teenager understand how they fit into a group, what their roles can be, is very valuable. If you take a group of teenagers in a teenage class and you have them choreograph a fight scene, and you don't tell them what their roles should be, you will find that there will be some who gravitate towards doing the movements, others who will come up with ideas, others who connect those ideas into the choreography. Allow them to test and experiment with how they define their roles in these groups. These are the challenges they crave, and this class is a healthy environment where you can help guide them in their journey to becoming a mature adult.

One of the questions that comes up when we talk about this is whether a teenage class should use traditional uniforms as most schools do in all their classes, or should they be permitted to wear street clothes? There is an upside and a downside to both. If you've ever heard kids talk about the way uniforms in a private school impact them, a lot of them like uniforms because they don't have to worry about what to wear, and there is no shaming over certain clothing. On the other side, martial arts uniforms are not great at flattering overweight bodies, and with much of the population being overweight these days, giving them the ability to wear street clothes can help them feel more comfortable. You have to decide what is right in your school.

In the end, when I look at this option, this idea of bringing more teenagers into a class, even giving them their own time and space at a school, this is one of the things that excites me most about martial arts and what we could do to help it grow. How many people start as children and then stop training? What if we had an entire generation of martial artists who started as children and *didn't* stop training? How good would martial arts get? How wonderful would our instructors be? Instead of reinventing the wheel and having a minute percentage of the population continue in martial arts training, martial arts could be the dominant, impactful pursuit in the world.

Teaching is a necessary part of martial arts education.
Anyone who has spent time teaching something knows
that they learn just as much,
if not more,
than the people they are teaching.

Part 10 – Basics

Basics

I find it funny how many people push back against training basics. There is nothing more fundamental than training your fundamental, basic movements. If we imagine a pyramid, where do basics go? They are at the bottom. Something fundamental could also be foundational. Think about that word, foundational. Foundation, the thing on which everything else is built. If your basics are terrible, everything else you do in martial arts will be terrible. How high can you build a house with a shaky foundation? Not very high.

The very best martial artists understand the importance of basics and routinely drill their basic movements. They find new and creative ways to incorporate them into their training, and if you are an instructor, and you understand the basics, you find new and creative ways to help your students train basics. The key to training basics and getting the most out of them is to avoid getting bored. If we practice our basics poorly or with low energy, we could even regress. Just because you do something doesn't mean you get better at it. You have to do it better to progress.

Here are 12 drills that you can use to train basics. You can drill them on your own, or you can train them in classes.

1. You can do your basics standing in place. Some basics work well with this, and others become challenging. Challenging is good.
2. You can practice them moving. Imagine all the different stances you know, and then incorporate

different hand and foot techniques, even combinations of them. Every technique has advantages and disadvantages. Different stances lead to more advantages and disadvantages. Combinations work well from some stances but not from others. If you think about all the techniques that you know, and then all the different combinations you could execute using those techniques, it's a really large number.

3. You can practice with your eyes closed. This is easy standing in place, but once you start moving, this becomes really challenging, especially if you have obstacles to consider.

4. You could practice in front of a mirror. One of the great values of working out in front of a mirror is that you get to see how something feels correlated with how something looks. That can be tough to do unless you have someone videotape you.

5. You can throw techniques at a target, whether you are coming close or hitting it.

6. Try all different sorts of targets: heavy bags, standing bags, the wall, etc.

7. You can practice those same techniques for speed.

8. You can practice them on a moving target.

9. Turn them into a cardiovascular workout.

10. You can throw them very, very slowly, with or without tension. Imagine taking 30 seconds to throw a single punch. What is that going to feel like? If you don't know, try it.

11. You can practice visualizing things. Try visualizing yourself doing it exceptionally well, visualizing a fight, imagining mystical battle, much like a video game, where energy is popping out of your hands.
12. Lastly, make forms out of your techniques. Imagine taking the structure, the movements, and the stances from any of your forms, and imagine you only get to use one technique. Go through your first form and only throw a backfist, for example. That is going to get weird, but you may find ways to use a backfist that you had never considered.

The better we get as martial artists, the more important it becomes to revisit our basic movements. The more time you spend working on your fundamentals, the better a martial artist you are. The better your technique, the better your sparring, the better your forms, the better your self-defense. No matter what you do, if your techniques are better, you and what you do are better.

We learn techniques so we can form concepts.
And then those concepts dictate our techniques.

Part 11 – Forms

The Importance of Forms

Martial arts forms are important. I know some people disagree with that. I'm going to give you ten reasons why they are. While I will accept that they don't have to exist in everyone's martial art curriculum, I think they should.

1. Forms help develop muscle memory for techniques, combinations, and stances. If you drill the same combination over and over and over again, that's essentially a form. By constructing a form that everyone learns and does on their own and is expected to know, you are encouraging people to learn martial arts in a certain way. Certain techniques are core to whatever style you train, and those forms reflect that.

2. It can help you develop your movements outside the pressure of sparring. Sparring can be very intimidating. Forms? Not so much. Once someone has a form down, they can practice putting in a lot of speed, power, etc. There are a lot of aspects they can incorporate into their forms training, and they don't have to worry about getting hit.

3. You can practice forms on your own, but you can't spar on your own. You can do freeform sparring, shadowboxing, punching a bag, or something similar, but having structure is important to develop certain things.

4. Forms offer variety. I know plenty of people who don't do well with sparring but do very well with forms. I know people who get bored with basics, but somehow when you construct that sequence from their techniques, they find their own space in it, and they do well.

5. There are a lot of ways you can do forms that are exciting. How often do we evaluate our basics in the same way we evaluate our forms? It adds a different dynamic to what we are doing, and that difference can be very fun.

6. Forms training can help develop the physical aspects of the martial arts, of your body. Deep stances, holding those stances, powerful techniques, fast techniques, slow techniques, these things are generally incorporated into forms. Maybe not all of them are in every form, but all of them tend to exist across all forms that a particular school might have. By training them, you develop your body.

7. It can also develop non-physical aspects. If you ask someone to do a particular form 10 times, one of two things will happen. They will get very bored, or they are going to learn to focus, to be present. Developing those non-physical aspects in martial arts is critical to the personal development side. I don't know how you do that more effectively than with forms.

8. Forms training gives you an opportunity to think about the practical application of the techniques we

do, whether you call it bunkai from Karate or you have a different term for it, that practical application, that self-defense side, that is something that interests a lot of people. To take a form and understand how those movements could apply, even if they are not completely or directly applicable, is a conversation you can have within your martial arts school to help people understand how things might actually go.

9. Forms offer common ground among martial arts schools and styles. I get excited when I go to a competition and see someone doing a form that I know, even if it's a different version. I've seen conversations and even friendships start because someone watched someone else do a form they knew. How cool is that?

10. Doing forms can help you enhance your central nervous system. By training these techniques in these ways repeatedly, pushing the boundaries of strength and speed, your body starts to adapt, and you become a stronger, faster, more efficient, better-reacting martial artist. I know of no other way to better work on this than with forms.

Drills

Just like with basics, there are a lot of different ways you can practice forms. It is important to break down a form and practice it in different ways because they are complex. If you don't believe that even a basic form can be complex, ask a very high-ranking, very skilled martial artist to do their most basic form. There is a lot in there. There is a lot of power and nuance, and you develop that nuance by training in different ways and training over time. Let's talk about 25 drills you can do.

1. You can do your form with your eyes closed.
2. You can face different directions. Often, we are conditioned that, "When I do this move, I am facing this part of the wall." It's good to know how to do that form facing anything.
3. You could do the form backwards, starting with the last movement and ending with the first movement.
4. You could do it mirrored. A lot of forms step out to the left. Step out to the right. Do everything in a mirror image.
5. What if you combine the two, mirrored and backwards?
6. If you are teaching a class, you could line everyone up. Have the first person do the first move and only the first movement. The second person only does the second movement. Continue in this way around

the class and watch people's brains explode. It's super fun!

7. Just do the hand portions in a form.
8. Just the foot portions.
9. No hands or feet, just the stances.
10. Do the form as slowly as possible. Take several minutes to get through the form. It can be exhausting, but it can also help you understand certain transitions.
11. Do the form as fast as possible.
12. Do it as strong as possible and put as much power into the techniques as you can possibly imagine.
13. Use as little energy as possible.
14. Do all of the movements but focus on the stances. How amazing can you make those stances? Deep, long, whatever those stances are supposed to be in that form, maybe even exaggerate it beyond what they are supposed to be.
15. You could exaggerate all of your motion. Your punches and kicks become really big, they reach out too far, your stances are huge, even difficult to move from one stance to the next.
16. If you are familiar with the Karate form Sanchin, you could apply that to any form. Do your form with as much tension across your entire body as possible. This is exhausting and very time-consuming, but very rewarding.
17. Do it in a confined space. In how small of a space could you do a form? Could you do it in a ten-foot box? Five-foot box? Two-foot box?

18. Do it on uneven ground. Find a hill. How would you do that form on a steep hill, facing in all the different directions you could?

19. Do it in water. Go to a beach or river, go into the water up to your waist, do that form. How is it different if you do it in water at knee level? Neck level?

20. Hold your breath. Can you do that form well holding your breath the entire way? You probably have to relax to do it.

21. Think about the application of every single movement. What are you doing when you do that form?

22. Do your form starting and stopping on the same spot on the floor. Maybe even put down a little piece of tape or a sticker.

23. Pick a sequence in the form and just work on that set of three to five movements. Drill those over and over and over again. This can be effective if there is part of your form that needs work.

24. This is one of my favorite ways to teach forms. Do the first move. Then do the first two moves. Then do the first three moves. Then do the first four moves, etc. As an aside, if you are teaching a new form with this method, you probably want to do more than one repetition per movement. I might do the first movement five times, then the first two movements five times. I've seen people learn forms in ten minutes in this way.

25. You could do the same thing but in reverse. Do the last movement. Then do the last two movements, and so on.

As important as forms are, coming up with different ways to do them makes them more exciting. It allows you to work on your forms more frequently. Let's face it, not everyone enjoys forms, and that's okay. As an instructor, having more drills available that help people get better at forms brings variety into your classes and gives you the opportunity to work on forms more frequently. Who knows? You might find some of the people who don't like forms like some of these drills, and the goal is that as they start to get better at them, maybe they even start to like forms.

Kiai

In most martial arts systems, there is some kind of yell. It could be called a kiai, a kihap, a spirit yell, a shout. Different schools and different styles call them different things, but most of us know what they are. It's some kind of energetic yell, a projection of energy, but it's not a grunt. Grunting is different. You are trying to take the energy from within your body and move it outside of your body in a way that others can hear, and if you're doing it well, even feel because sound creates vibration.

They don't always have to make noise. You can do this kiai - the term I'm going to use because it is the most universally understood - silently. A silent kiai is a very forceful exhale. It doesn't have to be loud. Of course, loud kiais are the most popular these days. It is what we see in competition, it is generally valued in most martial arts schools, and who doesn't want to make a big, loud noise that others can not only hear but feel? I love a good kiai.

In Judo, a kiai is used to intimidate, to express confidence. In Kendo, as with most martial arts, it can be part of an attack. By exhaling in this way, you can tighten the muscles in the diaphragm. It can reduce the damage taken if you get hit in that space while you kiai. Therefore, a lot of schools teach you to breathe out when you are hit. If you breathe out forcefully at the right moment, it's not going to hurt as much, maybe even not at all.

A properly done kiai doesn't come from the throat. It doesn't come from the vocal cords. It comes from the diaphragm. It comes from deep within you, and it projects outward. In order to do them properly, you have to understand breathing, and you have to be confident in projecting that force. You are not tightening the muscles in your throat; you are tightening the muscles in your gut.

Everyone's kiai is different. When done properly, your kiai is going to sound different than the others in your school, and it is important to understand that. A fair amount of people mimic kiai, but you can't have a good one unless you are truly embracing it as your own. If your kiai is high-pitched, if it is deep, if it rattles, own that. Just as your voice is different, and your body is different, your kiai is different. It's the only way to do it, so welcome it.

Understanding the Space Between Movements

When you start out in martial arts, you spend a lot of time not only memorizing the forms but learning how to manipulate your body, how to get from A to B, this stance to that stance, how to move forward and back, certain punches, etc. As you get better, you start to focus on certain things that are specific to that form. Maybe there is a challenging kick combination in a particular form, or how to get from this stance to that stance quickly, but if you watch two really good martial artists compete, and if they are doing the best forms they can do, and one of them is clearly better than the other, it is usually because of one thing, and that is something that I very rarely see written or talked about. It is their ability to work on the space between movements.

Any decent musician can play a note, even a sequence of notes, but the best musicians know how to play the space between the notes. Being a great martial artist is the same. A truly great form doesn't ignore the space between the movements - the timing, the breathing, the tension. There are a lot of ways you can present that space. How long does it take you to go from this movement to that movement? Where are your eyes? What is your posture? What is the energy you put off? It is the space between movements that allows martial artists to individualize their forms. When I'm taught a form, if I'm going to do it properly, I have to do certain movements in a certain order. Even in schools where the timing between movements is prescribed, I can still do certain things on my own. Maybe that is the muscles that are tight versus relaxed. Maybe it is my breathing. Every school is different, so I don't want to say what is done at yours is universal, but rather there is always a way to find that space and make it your own.

When you present a form, whether it is in class or at a competition, you are acting. You are showcasing a battle that you are in, and hopefully, winning. If you become more confident in your form, the presentation of that form will look better. Thus, your martial arts will get better. In a previous section, we talked about drills to help you get better at your forms. Those slower aspects, some of those drills that involve moving very slowly or very intentionally, will give you the time to consider how that space between the movements looks. What is it you are trying to accomplish? What is the vibe you are trying to present here? Is this an intense, angry, jittery sort of form, or is it calmer and more relaxed, with quiet confidence? You can do the same movements in the same way and just change the space between and get a very different result.

Some say that martial arts progress from kihon (basics) to kata (forms) to kumite (sparring). But I reverse the last two. I've seen plenty of poor martial artists who know how to fight. But everyone I've met that's excellent at forms has been, at least, a good martial artist overall.

Part 12 – Sparring

Overview

Sparring is an important part of martial arts. It bridges the gap from basics and forms to self-defense. When we think about self-defense, we're thinking about martial arts that have fewer rules. We're trying to get ready for a confrontation on the street. There are far fewer parameters to constrain us and the person or people that we are fighting against. On the other side, basics have a ton of rules. Forms have maybe even more. When we look at sparring, it occupies a space in between. Sparring is how we take our basics, make them our own, find out how they work, and prepare ourselves to let those rules, those parameters, fall away in a self-defense situation.

Part of martial arts is learning how to apply your techniques. Yes, martial arts is about personal development, but I feel pretty strongly that if you don't have the ability to defend yourself, even if it is just a slightly better chance of surviving a situation because of your training, then it's probably not a good martial arts curriculum. Part of understanding how to get better usually includes and probably should include some sparring. I'm not trying to come down hard on any schools that don't teach sparring, but I think you should.

Drills

There are a lot of ways that you can spar. Sparring drills fall into two different categories: drills that you can do by yourself and drills that require other people. Any drill that involves another person is going to be far more realistic, but let's face it, sometimes you don't have another person. Being able to drill your sparring and get better on your own is valuable.

Sparring itself can be intense, even if it is not physically intense. It can create a lot of anxiety for people, especially new martial artists. Coming up with some drills and having them as part of your curriculum, even if it's something that you do on your own because you're a student and not the instructor, can help you out tremendously. It can make your time sparring more productive.

Any sparring drills that you do with partners can be broken into four key areas:

1. Timing, where maybe you are practicing from a relaxed state or coordinating movements with your partner.
2. Accuracy, where you are focused on performing the right movement, or the right movement to a certain location or target.
3. Diversity, where you are trying to get better at using other movements. Most of us have a few core movements that we do repeatedly, but it's always

good to have more. One of the easiest ways to do this is to reduce the speed of your sparring.

4. Flow, not stopping your movement in order to think or react. If you are familiar with the drills sticky hands or chi sau, these are examples of flow drills.

Individual drills have the same four key areas: timing, accuracy, diversity, and flow. If you want to work timing drills on your own, there are random timer apps that can pop up and beep, and when that happens, you throw a technique. You are reacting to that stimulus of the beep. For accuracy, it's not that hard to hang a target, or maybe you have a heavy bag and you put some tape on it for a target. There are a lot of different, creative ways that you can get more accurate. One of my favorite ones, if you are practicing sparring that involves you trying to get close, especially to the face, use a wall. Do you know what happens when you punch a wall? It hurts! It's great training! Diversity could be shadow boxing, sparring on your own. If you have a mirror, all the better. For flow, shadow boxing can be used in this way, too. Spar for 30 seconds and don't stop moving at any point.

If you think about what you are working on in your sparring, and most of us know where we are struggling - if you don't, ask someone to watch you - you can break down some drills solo or with other people that help you get better at that skill. If you always back up when you are sparring, start with your back to the wall. You have to move to the side. If you do the same three or four techniques repeatedly, spar with someone who is high ranked, bring the speed down, and they are going to predict everything you throw. You'll have to change. Otherwise they will block 100% of your techniques. There are a tremendous number of sparring drills, more than we could ever incorporate into this book, so honestly, I'm not going to try.

The key to getting better at sparring is time and thoughtfulness. The more intelligent you are with your sparring drills, the better you'll be able to apply these new or refined skills in your actual sparring.

I love sparring. It's heaps of fun, and I think everyone should do it. The better you are at sparring, the more enjoyable it is. Sparring doesn't have to be anything. It doesn't have to be hard. It doesn't have to be fast. Sparring is simply working with other people in a freeform way. In fact, "freeform" isn't always the case. Sparring gives you an opportunity to better yourself and help other people get better, regardless of your rank or skill, so embrace it.

Treat your training partners with respect. They're giving you the gift of their body, so that you might get better.

Part 13 – Self-Defense

Fear & Anxiety

Stress has numerous benefits when it is in small amounts. Overall, a martial arts class is a pretty non-stressful environment, and yet when we get into self-defense situations, things change greatly because of stress. We, as human beings, react poorly when we are stressed. Think about the last time you had too much to do and you snapped at a friend or family member. That's stress. That's not you. That's not how you are. You reacted differently because you were stressed and that changed not just the way you acted, but literally the chemical structure in your brain.

How do we work with that? We practice martial arts to get better at these things. We can use increasing amounts of stress to condition us to get better so that stress response is reduced. Stress input must get ramped up over time. If you take a brand-new student and you throw them into a really stressful drill, they don't have the opportunity to get better. I can condition my hand slowly over time, but I can't put my hand into a blender. That's too much.

Stress really needs to be part of training. If it's not, you end up with people who have great skills but can't apply them when they need them. As I travel around, I get the opportunity to work with different people in different martial arts styles and different schools, and I have watched martial artists who have been training for 20 years, people with great technique, people who can even spar well, fall apart in certain drills just because there is a little stress involved. If you are not used to stress, and if you don't know how to act while stressed, you might as well be a white belt, at least in that way.

How do we get better? First, we accept that stress exists and is something that we need to learn how to deal with, and we accept that our movements while stressed will never be the same as when we aren't. A self-defense situation will never look like a form. It's never going to be your best or even a decent sparring match. It's going to be ugly and messy, and if you watched it later on tape, you'd probably be embarrassed. The ability to act in a stressful situation is far more important than the ability to use technique. When we talk about a self-defense situation, stress and stress handling are far more of a factor than the physical techniques we're talking about.

How do you adapt to stress? You find small amounts of stress. Stress tends to come from the unknown or the uncontrollable. If I walk up to you on the street and I tell you, "Hey, I'm going to mug you. I'm going to take my right hand and punch you right here. Three, two, one," you're probably going to be a little stressed, but more so confused. Why would I tell you this? If the same situation occurs, but I walk up to you and tell you, "Hey, I'm going to mug you. Give me your wallet, or I will hurt you," you're going to have a very different response. You're going to be stressed, and the way we act under stress is going to be different.

I'll share with you my favorite drill for enabling stress. This is the one that I teach when I travel around. I call it Dark Alley. This is not my own drill. This is something I have had in my toolbox that I learned many years ago. It goes like this: You take a group of people, split them in two, and you line them up facing each other with roughly four to five feet in between the rows. They don't have to be facing directly across from each other, they can be staggered, and there should be several feet between each person. You take one person, bring them up to the front and turn them around. You then walk through and designate some, but not all those people standing in lines as attackers. Those people get to throw a single slow attack. The person up at the front is then turned around and has to walk through that corridor of two lines of people. They have to defend those attacks, never knowing where the next random attack will come from.

This is the drill where I watch people fall apart, and I find it fascinating. We are taking out the predictability. They don't know who the attackers are, and they don't know what attack will be used. They do know they will be safe, and they do know it's a single attack, and that when they first start working with this drill, it will be slow. There is no risk, and yet the stress level is through the roof because of the unknown.

As people get better with this drill, you can increase the speed, and you can increase the other conditions. What if people throw more than one technique? What if two people can attack at one time? There are a lot of things you can do with this drill, and as you start to see the principles here, I'm sure you can come up with several other drills to create this stress response. As you drill it, you get better. As you get better, stress doesn't bother you as much. If someone attacks you on the street, you are going to be stressed, but learning how to work with it gives you a far better chance of the outcome that you want.

Instincts

Instinct is something that everyone has, but we don't all have it in the same degree. Some people have stronger senses. Whether you call that sixth sense or instinct, or however you choose to term it, it's something we all have, but most of us ignore. Instinct can be very useful in freeform movement, especially with a partner while sparring for example, but one of the things that is most challenging about our instinct and how to incorporate it into our martial arts is the fact that we don't fully understand what it is. It's there, but how do we use it?

Have you ever had a bad feeling about something? Have you ever thought, "Maybe I shouldn't go here today," but you had no reason why? That's instinct. If you spend much time on the internet, or even if you just talk to your friends, you can come up with plenty of examples where their instinct helped them, or they ignored their instinct, and something happened.

Instinct can help you anticipate a partner doing a movement they shouldn't. It can help you anticipate what's going to happen on your drive home. Maybe somebody is going to cut you off. You have no reason to know why, but you start to give space, and BAM, there's the car, and if you hadn't made space, it would have hit you.

Instincts can be developed, but the first step is to accept them, to honor them, recognize that you have them and that you value them. The next step to developing your instincts is to use them. Observe people, whether you are in a car, or at a coffee shop, or in class. Watching the way people act, the way they move, you'll start to get feelings. I know, we're getting a little woo-woo here, but you get these feelings tied to certain movements. You become more sensitive over time to those feelings. Those are your instincts.

To put it another way, trust your gut.

Avoiding Fights

The only way to win a fight is to avoid it entirely. The best way to avoid a fight is to avoid dangerous situations, locations, and people. To say it another way, don't go to dumb places with dumb people and do dumb things. Anywhere alcohol exists carries an increased opportunity for dumb things to happen. I'm not saying you shouldn't go places that have alcohol. I'm saying you should be aware, you should trust your instincts, and you should be observant when you are in these places.

Everywhere you go, everything you do carries a risk, and you must consider that risk. You've got to pick your battles. If your gut tells you that going to a certain place this evening is likely to result in something negative happening, is it worth going there? Can't you go somewhere else? If you chose to ignore that instinct, be more aware.

Whenever something looks like it is about to happen, there is almost always time to diffuse the situation. Fights rarely come completely at random. It does happen, but it's hard to prepare for those things, so we prepare for what we can. You can generally diffuse a situation before it escalates. Try to talk people down. Be humble. If that doesn't work, walk away. If you can't do that, crack a joke, especially at your own expense. If none of that works, be crazy. People don't want to fight with someone they think is insane. Lastly, be gross. Blow your nose in your hands. Spit on your hands. There are other even grosser things that I won't get into. People don't want to mess with someone so crazy that they are willing to be disgusting. Are these strategies guaranteed to deescalate a situation? No. Nothing is, but the more effort you make, the less likely something is going to turn into a fight.

When people tell me their stories about fights, I'm never impressed by the fights that they win. It's the fights that never happened, the ones that looked like they were inevitable, but somehow, they found a way to talk themselves out of it. That's what I find most impressive. To me, that is true self-defense.

Tools

There are a lot of tools you can use within self-defense. Most martial arts have some form of weaponry available. In a lot of schools, the bo or the staff is the first weapon that is learned, because what is it? It's a big stick, and you can usually find a big stick anywhere: a pool cue, a broom handle, etc. It's basic. One of my favorite things about it, especially when I'm teaching new students, is that it's hard to hurt yourself with a stick that you hold with both hands.

Knives are very versatile. Many of us carry them daily, even if we're not thinking of carrying them as a weapon because they are multipurpose tools. Learning how to use a knife is incredibly valuable. Everyone recognizes that a knife is a weapon, and that is its major downside.

As an alternative, you have things like palm sticks or kubotan, and those have some advantages. Those are not obviously knives. They are not detectable in metal detectors, so they are not going to attract attention. While they will inflict pain, they probably will not kill anyone. It's hard to argue that a small stick is a weapon you possess with the intent to murder someone. If things get to the point of legal situations, if you get sued because someone tried to harm you and you defended yourself, they are not going to be able to make a strong case that this stick you had in your pocket was there with the intent of killing them. You might also carry a pocket flashlight or a durable pen. Those can be used similarly to a kubotan or palm stick.

Next up is canes. The cane is a wonderful weapon, as much as very few of us are going to carry it because no one suspects it as a weapon. In the United States, the Americans with Disabilities Act prevents anyone from telling you that you can't carry it. It is pretty much the only weapon you can carry on a plane, and I know martial artists who carry it on a plane for that reason.

A piece of chain or rope can be useful if you know how to use it. What about your shoes? As martial artists, we don't tend to think of our shoes as weapons, but if you get really good at kicking something hard with your barefoot, and then you put a surface like a shoe over it, it can do even more damage. How about the rubber sole scraping down someone's shin? Oh, that hurts! There are things you can add to your shoes to reinforce them. There is a product out there that I have no affiliation with called Kuba-Kickz. It's a hard piece of plastic that threads through your shoelaces over your shoe. Depending on the pants that you wear, it might not even be visible, but when you go to kick someone, it adds a great deal to your kick. Then you've got things that similarly enhance the fingers: brass knuckles, key rings, key chains, even a ring with a point on it could do a lot of damage.

I'm not suggesting that you turn your body and your pockets into a rolling arsenal of martial arts weaponry, but if the idea of carrying one or more of these things makes you feel more confident, and you project that confidence as you walk about during your day, you are less likely to have to deal with a situation. People who target others are generally looking for an easy target. If you are confident, you are less likely to appear as an easy target.

Movements that Don't Injure

Most of the time, when martial artists teach self-defense, we teach these traumatic movements, and we talk about how dangerous they are, "Be careful because this could kill people." What about the other end of the spectrum? What about movements that are simply deterrents that extract you from situations? These are my favorite movements.

Many people struggle with violence, especially if they are not people who are in martial arts for self-defense. What if you are teaching a self-defense seminar? Teaching people to poke someone in the eyes or claw at the throat, that is not something for which everyone has the proper mindset. To ignore that, or simply say, "If they're in a self-defense situation, they'll get over it," that is ignoring the reality. That doesn't always happen, especially considering that a lot of people aren't going to go there until they know they need to, and by that time it's too late.

The very nature of defending yourself before it's too late means you're probably escalating the level of violence. That carries legal risk, and it counters a lot of psychology that we have in civilized society, not to mention the anxiety of self-defense in a real-world situation. This stuff gets messy and not just mentally and emotionally but physically.

What about having some movements at our disposal that don't cripple people, that you don't have to wait until the last moment to deploy, movements that if you move and you were wrong, you are simply embarrassed? I'll give you some examples. If someone comes up and bear hugs you from behind and you don't know who it is, you've got some options. You could stomp on their foot, and you could elbow them if you have enough movement in your arms, you could take your heel and drag it down their shin, maybe if it's a man, grab their groin.

What if it's just as likely to be a stranger as it is to be a friend you haven't seen in a long time? If you just reach down and pinch the inside of their thigh, it startles people. They tend to release, at least enough that you might be able to get out, push away, turn, and see what you are dealing with. If you are facing the person or have reach, slowly, gently pushing up under someone's nose can help. I've never seen anyone who can resist this. I have taken the biggest, strongest people I know and demonstrated this movement. I just apply pressure underneath their nose with a single finger, and it moves their head back. The moment their head moves back, they don't have good balance, they can't see what is going on, and anything else that they would want to do changes.

Try taking a couple of fingers and slowly pushing them into someone's throat, the bottom of the throat, that soft spot. With even a little pressure it can start to affect your ability to speak. This can be effective. It's uncomfortable. No one likes that, but I didn't damage anyone. I'm not going to jail for it.

The last example I'll give, one that is kind of ridiculous, but at the same time, if you know me, you know why I'm including it here, is a Wet Willy. To wet your finger and stick it in someone's ear is disgusting, and if you don't know the person doing that do you, you are probably going to lose focus of whatever it is you were doing. Bonus points if you do both ears at once!

Why are these moves so important? It is because people have a hard time escalating violence. What if you are attacked by someone that you don't actually want to hurt? What if someone in your family is really drunk, they've been through a divorce or something really rough, you can empathize with them, and they are not trying to kill you, but they are mad, and you know that seriously injuring them is not the direction you want to take? Having moves like this is important. For any of you who have say over a martial arts curriculum, incorporating movements like this and teaching them as the most fundamental movements is very important. The most critical thing about self-defense is not getting into difficult situations. The second most critical thing is being able to get out of any situation regardless of the degree to which we are threatened. Only after movements like this don't work should we be considering real violence and hurting people.

Balancing Safety with Effective Training

Safety and effective self-defense training are on opposite sides of the martial arts spectrum. If the only self-defense drills you do are completely safe, you are not preparing for the real world. If the only self-defense drills you do carry a tremendous amount of risk, people aren't going to progress and get better because they are going to be stressed. Finding a balance between the two, doing drills from across that spectrum, is important. It's about calculated risk because everything has risk. When you get in the car and drive to the grocery store, there is risk. It's fairly low versus the alternative of never buying food and thus never eating. Self-defense training is the same. We must find ways to mitigate that risk. The greater the risk, the greater the reward, but that's a moving target. If it's neither safe nor effective, DON'T DO IT. It's not worth it.

Everyone's tolerance for risk is different, and that is okay. As a martial arts instructor, helping people train in drills that will be effective for them, even if the risk is a little more than they are comfortable with, is important. Maybe you find a way to make the drill safer for that person, or maybe you slow down the speed, so they are less threatened, less scared, or maybe they watch the first few times you do that drill. There are multiple ways you can handle it, and it depends on why they are not comfortable with that drill.

Every self-defense drill should have a goal, and the goal of every drill is probably different. We want to make sure we have drills that are appropriate for people's experience, skills, and age. It shouldn't just be based on rank. To put a very, very fine point on it, if you are training rape defense in a martial arts school, and you know that one of your students has been raped, the way you handle that situation with them is different than the way you would handle that situation with someone who may not have had that experience. The way you would address that scenario with a 12-year-old is different from the way you would address it with a 40-year-old.

How do you mitigate risk? Start with proper communication, making sure everyone knows the parameters, the goals, the things to watch out for during the drill. The riskier the drill, the more important is it that there is someone on the outside observing it who has the ability and willingness to stop it at a moment's notice. In most cases, that is going to be the instructor, but not always. Safety equipment can also help mitigate risk.

You have to identify the problematic students. Some people get a little too juiced up in these real-world scenarios, and sometimes those people need different parameters. I'm thinking of a particular student right now, someone who has something to prove every time we get into a real-life scenario. Everyone understands that this is going to happen, and we continually talk to them, and they continue to struggle, but it's not my school, so I don't get to say what to do. What would I do? I would force them to go slower because speed is almost always the culprit when people start breaking parameters of any drill.

If it's a drill where you have to match people up, being intelligent about the groups or pairs that you set up will help mitigate risk. You must consider all factors, not just rank and size. Consider everything from strength, experience, willingness to participate in the way that it is given, emotional state, etc.

You have to maintain a proper atmosphere. If you remain calm in the way you present a drill and oversee a drill, people are more likely to hold to the paraments. If you get loud, excited, and yell, you are bringing everyone's energy up. They are more likely to make mistakes. You want to make sure that people have the freedom to try and to make errors, within reason and the parameters of the drill. Staying calm helps with that.

Find ways to reduce ego. If you tell someone they did a good job, tell them why. Don't reward people simply being dominant because they are bigger or stronger, because that inspires smaller, weaker people to escalate to seek praise.

You want to set goals. Make sure everyone understands the goals not only of the drill but of their personal participation in that drill. "Hey, Joe, when you step into this drill today, I want you focused on (x)." Give them something to think about. You can't think about everything at once, so pick one thing.

Err on the side of caution. If there are different ways that you can implement a drill, start with the least risky ones, because quite often, students will push the boundaries. They are going to escalate that drill for you, whether you want them to or not. If you start at the upper end and they push, that is where injuries happen, so start low. As they push, you push back. When they are ready, give them the next step. You escalate the drill and let them continue.

When we think about these drills, doing drills that are ineffective or always on the safe side of the spectrum doesn't do your students any good. You want to make sure that people can explore self-defense in a way that is as realistic and safe as possible. By doing this, you are preparing them for what might happen when you are not around. Be smart about that, be respectful of them, and of the martial art you are teaching. Martial arts and self-defense aren't the same, even though they have some overlap.

If you are a school that focuses on self-defense, you probably already do all of this. If you are a martial arts school, I encourage you to take a step back and look at what you teach as self-defense. Is it realistic? Is it helpful? Do you have confidence that your students are more likely to survive an outcome because of what you teach them? How much more? If your self-defense programs need work, there are scores of services out there. I'm not going to endorse any of them, but I would encourage you to take a look at them or to talk to other martial arts instructors that you know. How did they handle this? This is a group effort because overcoming violence is something for which we all have a passion. Maybe we don't all have an extreme passion, but I've never met a martial arts instructor who didn't care about keeping their students safe. By putting in some time and some effort, and increasing your education, you can have an even greater impact.

The only way anyone ever "wins" a fight is avoiding it entirely. And in that case, everyone wins.

Part 14 – Personal Development & Mindset

Dealing with Setbacks

The very best martial artists seem to be the very best at handling adversity. Life is hard. It's full of setbacks. If you listen to Martial Arts Radio, you know that in almost every episode, we hear some dramatic story about something that held our guest back, whether from their martial arts, maybe their personal life, or maybe their career. We all face these challenges.

I don't use the word failure when I teach, because what is a failure? The word failure means there is something final about it. There are no other options, you can't keep going, or you've stopped trying. In martial arts, there are always options. You never fail. You might not get that movement right at that time, but you can keep trying.

There are always ways to get better, always ways that we can move forward. As you train, you might not find the best option, but if you continue to find bad options and not repeat them, you eventually discover some things that do work.

I have some advice for dealing with setbacks. Choose your language carefully. Stay positive. Positivity is the key to overcoming any setback. If you believe you can, there is a chance. If you believe you can't, you never will. If your setback came as the result of a mistake, apologize. If you've harmed someone else, literally or figuratively, apologize to them directly. If you harmed yourself, apologize to yourself.

Treat yourself with the same kindness and respect that you would treat others. Know when to say when. If we are talking about your physical body, and it is injured, training through that may or may not be a good idea. Don't let your ego get in the way because a physical setback if dealt with improperly can become something more permanent or more severe. If the goal is to train as much as possible, taking a little time off now is better than taking a lot of time off later.

I've had plenty of adversity in my life. Quite a few people who should have been in my corner, supportive, helpful, told me that not only I couldn't but I shouldn't, why bother trying? People that you would have expected to have my back actually plotted my downfall. It hurts, but I've used that adversity, those naysayers, as fuel. I'll prove them wrong, and I've done that loads of times throughout my various careers. With whistlekick, there are people who have said this business would never work. In almost every case I've shown them that what they said would never work will and has.

There are lots of reasons to get up in the morning and dedicate yourself to certain things, and proving others wrong, depending on your personality type, can be very valuable. Whatever the setback you face, take it as a challenge. Take it as a lesson. There is always a learning opportunity no matter what we do, so if you can find the lesson in whatever it is you are facing, it makes it worthwhile, or at least not as negative as it otherwise might be.

Comparing Yourself to Others

Martial arts is a personal journey, yet somehow it becomes really instinctive to compare ourselves to others. There is an abundance of comparison that happens in society, and we bring it into our martial arts training. To a certain degree, even the rank structure that we have encourages comparison. Unfortunately, in most cases, we tend to value the personal journey less than the skill that people have.

When we think about where people started, the people that make the greatest progress may not be at the greatest standing. People who start with a physical advantage often have the opportunity to go further. Remember that people progress in different ways. Not everyone is comfortable or even able to grow rapidly. Sometimes people plateau and then take a big jump, others are slow and steady, and some people even regress as part of their journey and then progress again. The point is that our journeys are different because *we* are different. We have different experiences, different genetics, and different goals.

It is very tempting as we compare to look at someone else, then look at ourselves and say, "If I had what they have, I would be...," or "I could be better or more if..." Stop comparing yourself to others. Compare yourself to only one person, and that person is you. Have you moved forward? Have you gotten better? Is the you of today better in some way than the you of yesterday? I'm not necessarily talking about skill, because sometimes skill fades, but are you a better person? Are you a better martial artist? However you define that term, you probably are if you are spending your time training. If you are, that's all that matters.

If you are a good example for what a martial artist is, if you make the world better, if you contribute, if you take the lessons that you learn out into the world and make those around you better or at least happy for your presence, then you are setting an example of what a martial artist can be, and you are encouraging others to step into the martial arts and grow because of you. That is all I could ever ask of anyone else.

The "Right" Way

Some people believe that there is a single right way to do things. Guess what? They are wrong. There is more than one right way. In fact, there is *no* right way, and if there is no right way, then there is no wrong way.

What do I mean by that? If I value self-defense skills, and I am training in a soft style, like say, Tai Chi, that's probably not the best choice because my actions and my goals aren't aligned. You could say that's wrong, but maybe I am older, I have some health issues, maybe I value breathing and soft movement, or maybe the aggressive format of most martial arts does not work for me because of any number of reasons. In that case, Tai Chi might be the exact right option because my goals and my actions are aligned.

This whole "My martial art is better than your martial art" thing has become such a cliché, and it is holding back martial arts growth. To say something is right or wrong requires an expression of value. Values aren't the same for everyone. To pretend that they are is just arrogant. If I choose to live out in the woods, and you choose to live in the city, you can't say that my choice is wrong. It might be wrong for you, but it would be wrong for me to live in the city. On a personal note, I DO live in the woods. I choose not to live in the city because it would be wrong for me because of the things that I value.

Martial arts and martial arts styles are the exact same thing. Right and wrong are irrelevant because they don't exist. When we talk about techniques or forms, the idea that there are a right and wrong way is a myth. It is so incredibly subjective. Different schools have their own versions of different forms. To say, "This is the correct version of this form," why does one person get to decide that? Why is that person the final arbiter of all ways to do that form? Within a martial arts school, there may be a curriculum, and there may be a defined way to practice that form. That is the correct way to do that form in that school. That's fine. There are parameters that are set up because that school values that curriculum. The people who participate and train at that school value that curriculum, but if you are not part of that curriculum, that value doesn't exist, so you can't say that this is the right way to do this form.

Differences aren't bad. They are good! Celebrating the differences between martial arts is something we should be doing. They allow us to grow. If we were all doing the same thing, not only would it be boring, there would be no growth. As people practice different things in different ways, they discover new ideas, they test them, and then we explore them and incorporate the best. Every martial art practiced today originated in this way. No one woke up one day, developed a martial arts curriculum in a vacuum, and put out these movements that somehow worked. They incorporated movements that multiple people taught them.

I love seeing this evolution of martial arts, and if we can get rid of this "right and wrong" stuff, we will see even greater evolution and more progress. Imagine where we could be if we hadn't spent the last few decades here in this country tearing each other down. "This martial art is right." "This martial art it wrong." Now, I understand, there is a certain element of humanity in this. This is something we naturally do. We want to believe that what we do is worthwhile, and thus we extend that worthiness to say that what we do is right. If we look at something else, we try to say that it is wrong because it validates our investment in what we have done.

Martial arts today, in some schools, includes at least an acknowledgment of firearms. One hundred years ago, firearms didn't exist, at least not in the way that we have them today, with people able to carry them around on their hip, so there was no need to include firearms in a self-defense curriculum. Would it have been appropriate to say including firearms defense as part of a self-defense curriculum is wrong? It may not be traditional, and if you value tradition over other things, then maybe you could say it is wrong, but as long as we remember that values are more important than trying to create some objective right or wrong within the martial arts, we will be fine.

Martial arts is practically a living thing. It evolves, it changes, it interacts with others, with itself, and it is our job to foster it, to help it grow. To say that there is a right way is to stifle the progress of martial arts. I would love it if I could pass on to the next life, and let's say I get to look back in 100 or even 500 years. I don't want to see that martial arts are the exact same then as it is now. I want to see that is has grown and adapted because people will be different. We will be different sizes and shapes. We will have discovered different things about nutrition that allow our bodies to be different, and thus our martial arts have to be different. Our cultural needs for martial arts will be different, so the way we train and what we train should also reflect that.

Why People Struggle with Things that Have No Endpoint

One thing that is difficult about martial arts is that it has no end, and people have a hard time with things that don't end. People diet for fixed periods of time, but they have a hard time when it comes to making a permanent change to the way they eat. The reason people struggle with that nutrition is the same reason people drop out after earning a black belt. They see that as the endpoint. To be honest, many of us have conditioned the world to believe that earning a black belt is the endpoint.

What is ironic about this is that happiness rarely comes from achieving a goal. It comes from embracing the progress - from the process if you will. If you can find enjoyment in the learning of martial arts, the participation, and the practice, that is far more sustainable than doing something you don't enjoy because there is a certain color belt at the end.

When we are white belts, we look at that black belt and see that as the pinnacle, the endpoint, the goal. That is where we are trying to get. If you ask someone their goal in martial arts, it is quite often to earn a black belt, not to train for a certain amount of time, not to achieve a certain competitive outcome, but to earn a black belt. There was probably a time when, if asked, that would have been my goal, too. What is my goal today? It is to train for as long as I can and to learn as much as possible.

If we can detach praise, success, and education from rank, what we have is a much more sustainable pursuit. Martial arts is about personal development. Personal development shouldn't have an end. If I earn my black belt, and I have become a better person, and then I drop out, that is a shame. It's not bad, it's not wrong, but there is more. There is always more. I want people to get as much out of martial arts as they can.

Imagine a martial arts school with no rank. Everything else is done the same. It would still be worthwhile. If you are training, I hope you aren't training for rank. I hope you are training for any other reason. If you are training for rank, explore why. Is there something about your identity that you need the validation of rank? Explore that. Is there a way passed it? There probably is. If you are an instructor, help your students find value in things other than rank. In fact, make rank the least important part of the value they take from their training. You will have a more successful school. People will stick around far longer.

There are large numbers of people who have achieved very high ranks in the martial arts, and it becomes their identity. They introduce themselves as such-and-such rank at formal social gatherings. Some people look at that and say it is weird. Others look at it and say it is inappropriate. I look at it and think it is unfortunate because it becomes clear to me that all that person has in their life, the way they define themselves, is that rank. We should never define ourselves, even within our martial arts training, by a rank. Many and maybe even most of the very best instructors, yes, they use titles, but they contribute so much more than simply that title. They don't just observe and critique. They invest themselves in the education of others, and that can happen regardless of rank.

Meditation

Meditation, while it is not part of every curriculum or school, seems pretty tied into martial arts. Meditation is old, much older than I know. From my understanding of world religions, there is some aspect of something meditative in everyone. If martial arts does in fact stem from monks, then that might explain the connection - personal development through devout religious practice becoming devout physical practice. Countries that have strong martial arts cultures seem to have strong ties to religions that value meditation. It may be coincidence, I don't know, but I see quite a bit of synergy between meditation and martial arts.

Even if you don't see a synergy between the two, learning how to ignore distractions through meditation can be beneficial to your martial arts training. If you can focus, each repetition is going to be more impactful. You are going to get more out of everything that you do. Remember, it's not, "practice makes perfect." It's "perfect practice makes perfect," or to say it another way, "practice makes permanent," so you want to make sure that you are doing everything the best you can.

Meditation is being studied quite a bit these days, and we have seen some science that validates the benefits: relaxation, reduction of stress, improving concentration, increasing happiness, slowing aging, and improving both the cardiovascular and immune systems. These have all been documented. Meditation can help you develop faster reaction times by building your focus, to stay aware of everything that is going on, and only what matters. These all seem like good things to incorporate into our development. I don't know if it matters whether you consider it part of martial arts or separate. I include it here because I see value, and I see synergy.

Meditation can physically change the brain. It affects the thickness of the hippocampus, and with just a few weeks of meditative practice, you can positively alter your mind. I have participated in martial arts schools where meditation is part of the beginning and end of class, and I love that, because it allows me to focus my mind, let go of the world, to begin my martial arts training, and then at the end, to reflect on my training, what I learned, and start to acknowledge that the rest of the world does in fact exist.

You can meditate whenever you want. It can be separate or part of your martial arts practice. The key, like most habits, is doing it at the same time of day, every day, in a certain place. Be consistent. Everyone can find a couple minutes every day, so start there. Five minutes of meditation practice can go a long way. After you start to see the benefits, five minutes may turn into ten, or fifteen, or maybe even more. It doesn't have to take over your life, but it can certainly supplement it.

Self-Doubt

Self-doubt is going to creep into your life at some point, and it's probably going to be something you face in your martial arts. It is that feeling that you are inadequate: maybe you're not good enough to do this, maybe you should quit, stop bothering, you're never going to pass that belt test. Self-doubt comes because we care. There are plenty of things that I'm not good at that I never consider improving because I don't care about getting better at them. They are not part of my life that matters.

In order to feel inadequate, we have to set a standard, something that we are trying to reach or maintain, and feel like we aren't there; like we are not on track. That feeling of self-doubt can be depressing, crippling, and that fear of failure - you know from an earlier section how I feel about that word - can be so great for some of us that we never try. I tend to counter my feelings of inadequacy by working too much or too hard. The consequence of that is that it can backfire. Sometimes I get sick because I work too much, but there is value in these feelings of inadequacy because they show us what truly matters. The things that we value the most are the things that create these feelings. Too much self-doubt will restrict you from the life you want to live, so finding ways to overcome it, or at least work with it, is important.

How you handle these feelings, how you overcome them or work with them, depends greatly on who you are and what we are talking about. If we are talking about martial arts, maybe your feelings of inadequacy can be handled with some practice, or maybe talking to your instructor. Maybe it requires changing the goals. Maybe you wanted to learn a certain form by a certain date. Maybe you were unable to learn that form because maybe something came up. You might feel bad for not achieving that goal, but you can always rewrite the goal. You can still learn that form. Is it worth feeling poorly?

All we have is what we are going to do. Sure, memories and stories are important, but when we talk about progress, that is looking forward. How we have done and what we have done will shape what we can do, but we are not locked into it. We have options, and if we dwell on what we didn't do or how we didn't do it, we are locking ourselves in the past. The best way to solve problems that occurred in the past is to focus on the future because guess what? It's the only way. If I start training at a new school and everyone there is great at sparring, and I'm not so great at sparring - and yes, this is a real-world example that has happened to me - I have a couple things I can do. I can stop, or I can accept where I am, welcome the fact that I am so bad at something that there is so much opportunity for growth, and open myself up to getting better. Yes, that latter option is what I chose to do.

I don't know anyone who doesn't have feelings of self-doubt from time to time about at least one thing. I know that as I have gotten to know myself better, as I've come to understand my why, the reasons that I train, the better I have been at letting go of those feelings. Do I wish I trained more? Yes. Do I sometimes feel like I am a fraud because I don't train as much as I want? Yes, but I love to train, I love what it has brought me, and I love the martial arts, so I look at those feelings of self-doubt, the standards that I have set for myself, and I try to forget about the standards that others may set for me. I can't change other people's thoughts or actions, but I can change mine. I recognize that I am not going to be able to do everything, so I focus on what I can do. Do what you can, with what you have, where you are.

Martial Arts as Service

There are countless ways you can look at martial arts, especially the way you teach it or give back to it, but one of my favorite ways is to look at martial arts as service. Not *a* service, not in the sense that you are providing a service to others, but look at it such that you are serving, that you are giving back through not just instruction but your training overall. Sometimes the word service is used in a religious connotation. That is absolutely not what I am saying here. I'm talking about a mindset of service, the idea that by training you are doing something that is actually for someone else.

What about service as a mindset when you are training? Here are some ways you can look at it. If I go to a martial arts class, I am serving the instructor and other students. If I go to a martial arts competition and compete, I am serving the tournament promoter and other competitors. If I go to that same competition as a referee, I am still serving the promoter and competitors. I am helping to foster an environment that betters them. If I go to a seminar, I am serving the other attendees, the host, the guest instructors. Anywhere you are training; you are serving others. Even if you train at home by yourself, you are serving the people that you may train with in the future, you are serving the people you may defend in a self-defense situation, or at its most fundamental, you are serving every single person that you may come in contact with in a better way because you have grown personally through your martial arts training.

The opposite of serving others is serving yourself. It's the selfish way. I would say that most martial arts students are attending classes for selfish reasons. If you do this, I'm not saying you are wrong. The difference is in your accountability. You are accountable to yourself if your reasons are for yourself. Instead, if I am serving others, my accountability is to others. If I am serving in a class setting, I have to set a good example for everyone else. It's not about my ego. It's not about rank. It is about being the best example I can knowing that it impacts others and their training.

If you have been teaching martial arts for long, you know that one person who is fired up and ready to train can completely change the energy in a class and take what might have been a poor class or even a bad class and make it a great one. The ironic fact is that by focusing on serving others, we actually get more out of it ourselves. This is not some dramatic shift. This is already instilled in the culture of martial arts. I just don't hear it discussed.

If we change our priorities so that service becomes the goal, the entire class benefits. We are less likely to skip class, we are more likely to practice the things we don't do well, and we are more likely to have a great attitude. True service is done without expecting anything in return, so this service approach can make it easier to tolerate long droughts in between rank. It can help you handle the plateaus that inevitably come from long-term martial arts training.

Service to others affects the priority of your actions. I have gone to class simply because I know others will benefit from it. On days that I don't feel well, maybe it is too hot, or I have a million excuses why I don't have to go, shouldn't go, or don't want to go, I still go because I want others to benefit from my presence.

Are You a Martial Artist?

Am I still a martial artist if I stop training at a particular rank? If I take a single month of Krav Maga, am I a martial artist? If I stop training for a single year, am I still a martial artist? What if I trained for 50 years and then I stop for a year? Am I no longer a martial artist? What if I become injured, and I am limited to training the movements in my mind? Do I get to retain the title of martial artist?

Martial arts and being a martial artist defy any kind of objective definition. Martial arts is one of the most subjective things I am aware of, and because of that subjectivity, some of us will argue over it. I don't like to argue. I think it is a waste of time. I would rather spend that time training. In fact, the people that are arguing, I would rather they spent their time training, too.

If you define yourself as a martial artist, you should be living as a martial artist. Martial arts isn't what I do. It's not what anyone does. It is who they are. When you train for a long time, and you meet someone else who has trained for a long time, you can feel it. Martial arts leaves this indelible mark on your person, on your soul. It becomes core to who you are in a way that is practically genetic.

There are martial artists who become physically disabled, but do they stop being a martial artist? I don't think so. Their martial arts spirit helped them survive that situation. They have the strength to carry on. Maybe they can't do all the physical things they did, or maybe they can't do any of the physical things, but are they training in some way, even mentally? Are they working to become better through practice? Are they developing who they are personally? Then, yes, I would say they are still a martial artist.

I like to think of things, including being a martial artist, in terms of spectrums. One end of the martial artist spectrum is people who have never trained. No one has the right to tell someone that what they are doing is or is not martial arts. It is entirely subjective, and it has a place on that spectrum. If it works for you, and everyone involved in the equation is happy about it, you should do it. If you think of a style and say that is or is not a martial art, if everyone engaged in that practice is happy and benefits, it's irrelevant.

For me, a martial artist is someone who has trained physically in the martial arts recently -- however they define recently. It is someone that has every intention to engage in that physical practice again soon -- however they define soon. They are currently engaged in the application of the lessons that they have learned as a martial artist. Let me say those points a little less formally. You trained recently, you are going to train again soon, and you are trying to get better. That is what a martial artist is.

Martial arts can bring people together in a way that is so incredibly powerful. I am not aware of any other tool - by tool, I mean physical practice - that has helped more people on deep fundamental levels than martial arts. I wish everyone spent time training, even if it was temporary. Maybe everyone who trains can't refer to themselves as a martial artist for the rest of their lives, but they can still benefit from the time that they could. I am a martial artist, and I am proud to be one, and I hope that you are, too.

I *know of no greater tool for personal growth than traditional martial arts.*

Closing Thoughts

Everything about this book has been interesting. From the conceptualizing, to the work on it. The editing, the reconciling different opinions on everything from word choice and punctuation to larger concepts, and even definitions.

In those ways, writing a book is similar to martial arts training.

I want to make it clear that what is here contains nothing but my opinion. Yes, you'll likely find some facts in here. Maybe even numbers. But I'm not claiming that anything here is factual and backed up by science. It's opinion, based on experience and thought. If you feel differently, good. If something I'm asserting is untrue in your experience, I want to know about it.

While I've spent decades training, I'm not as skilled a writer. I'm not a white belt... but certainly not a black belt. The next iteration of this book will improve. Future books will be better. I intend to use my writing as both personal expression and growth opportunity. Thank you for indulging me in those areas.

I appreciate you taking the time to read this book, whatever your reasons may be.

Train hard, smile, and have a great day!

~jeremy

About whistlekick

You can find more about whistlekick, and everything we're doing, at whistlekick.com

And, yes, the w is meant to be uncapitalized.

Printed in Poland
by Amazon Fulfillment
Poland Sp. z o.o., Wrocław

63887955R00139